Your

PASSPORT

To

PROMOTION

11 PRINCIPLES TO ACCELERATE
YOUR CAREER AND SECURE THE
PROMOTION YOU DESERVE

ROBB D. THOMPSON

Your Passport To Promotion
ISBN 1-889723-69
Copyright © 2006 by Robb Thompson
Family Harvest Church
18500 92nd Ave.
Tinley Park, Illinois 60487

Cover and Text Design: Amanda Fico

Contents

Foreword

Finally someone has it right; in a world of pseudo rationale we are now presented with a handbook that can be carried with you as measurements against your daily progress.

Dr. Robert Thompson has achieved a classic self-help, useful, hands-on, ste-by-step, unfailing roadmap to obtain the level of excellence of success that for too long has remained a mystery. This is not just something that you read once and put it down, this is to be 'studied' on a continuous basis.

Peter J. Daniels

Constant Pursuit Is The Only Option

My passion is excellence. I press for it every day. I push for it. I pursue it. I desire it. I strive to find ways to become better in everything I do. I cringe at the thought of being the same tomorrow as I am today. Over the course of my life I have seen this to be true: **I will never possess what I am unwilling to pursue.**

> YOU WILL NEVER POSSESS WHAT YOU ARE UNWILLING TO PURSUE.

I'm not only interested in *myself* becoming a person of excellence. My desire is to help you rid your life of mediocrity as well. With easy to apply principles, you can reach a higher level of success and fulfillment than you have ever imagined. My desire is to help you to reach your highest possible potential!

It's important to have someone in your life who not only pushes you to go further, but also can take you to another level. Very rarely will you get there by yourself. Success is a team sport; no one climbs to the top alone. You need someone who is further along than you are, someone to put his hand on your shoulder and help you get where you want to go.

That is my desire — to help you focus on winning in life — spirit, soul, and body. Your past doesn't matter. You have greatness resident on the inside of you, and when you realize that, nothing and no one can stop you from achieving all your dreams and attaining the promotion you've always desired.

Rising to another level in the workplace doesn't just happen automatically or by chance. **Success is the result of choices not chances.**

> SUCCESS IS
> THE RESULT OF CHOICES
> NOT CHANCES.

Different choices take you down different paths. Wrong choices take you to places you don't want to go. Or you can choose *on purpose* to become everything you were destined to become!

Yes, that choice involves a great deal of change, which isn't always easy. But once you become willing to do whatever it takes to excel, *nothing* can hold you back — not vain pressures, nor another person's criticisms, nor any adverse circumstances assigned to trap you in the mire of mediocrity.

Please don't think for a minute that this book is just a nice little collection of platitudes I put together. Everything I share with you has already produced great dividends for me in my business dealings. If you could have seen me before I started implementing these principles, and then witness the life I live today, you would understand what I mean.

I understand the challenge of having to overcome a very difficult childhood. I know what it's like to be abused. Both my parents were alcoholics; I was too, by the age of thirteen. By the time I was sixteen years old, I was also a drug addict.

Be careful not to allow yourself the luxury of the excuse that your background or your childhood experiences are keeping you from success. I know you can do it, because I did it! I am determined to do whatever I have to do to reach the next level in every area of life. I refuse to allow myself to be mediocre. I know where I'm going. And today I am winning.

This is a choice you and I have to make for ourselves. You are personally responsible for your future. Decide what you want. Do you want to stay the way you are? It takes action to change, to make things different in your life. **If you don't do something to accelerate who you are, you'll likely never go anywhere.** If you just sit around and wait for others to do something for you, you'll end up very disappointed.

You are reading this book for a reason. One of the main reasons you may be reading is because you desire career success. You have a desire to be a success and maybe even move up the corporate ladder. I wrote this book for those very reasons. But more importantly, I want to deal with you. I want to show you how to function as a person of excellence in the workplace. My desire is to help you launch into the pursuit of achieving your full potential whether as an employer or an employee.

Winning in the workplace is simple, because there is actually very little competition. In fact, there is plenty of room at the top! The bottleneck of competition and struggle is at the bottom. If you can get past that bottleneck, you'll make it to the top.

From every direction imaginable, this modern generation is pressured to succumb to mediocrity. Many people have bought into the lies that they are victims; that they are the way they are because of someone else; that they should be paid a wage just because they show up to work. They are even convinced that neither the quality of their work nor their personal integrity really matters. Can you see this blatant deception?

You weren't designed to be mediocre, and you don't have to settle for second best. You don't have to remain where you are. You can excel at everything to which you diligently set your hand!

I want to help you understand not only how to cause doors of opportunity and promotion to open in your life, but also how to *keep* them open. It is time to go beyond worrying over how you're going to pay your next bill. Your life in the workplace can be one that goes from success to success, from promotion to promotion, and from victory to victory.

However, before that can take place, *a willingness to change is necessary*. A willingness to finally eject complacency from our personal and professional life! As you make the all important choice to follow the dynamic principles contained in this book, you'll experience great success. **Success and failure are destined to no one; they are destinations of a chosen path.** These truths will change not only your experience in the workplace — they will transform your entire life. Soon, people will identify you as a man or woman of success.

"TWO ROADS DIVERGED IN A WOOD,
AND I TOOK THE ONE LESS TRAVELED BY,
THAT HAS MADE ALL THE DIFFERENCE."

— ROBERT FROST

Determination:
Rising To Another Level

"JUST GOOD ENOUGH" IS NOT ACCEPTABLE BEHAVIOR TO A MAN OF EXCELLENCE.

Life was designed to be a continual ascension. Excellence is, by its very definition, *progressive*. You cannot expect your level of excellence today to continue over into tomorrow. In order to excel, we must be willing to change for the better.

So, no matter what level you are today, tomorrow you should be ready to move up to a higher one. You have been designed for movement and change!

Now, let's put this in the context of the workplace. You shouldn't let a day go by without looking for ways to become a better employee, employer, entrepreneur, or executive. **You can decide every single day to push away from mediocrity as you press toward the next level of excellence.**

> TODAY'S EXCELLENCE
> IS
> TOMORROW'S MEDIOCRITY.

Most people don't realize what it takes to achieve that next level. They think success in the workplace is some great unattainable mystery.

The truth is: **Most individuals aren't willing to make the sacrifices and changes that are necessary to propel them forward toward promotion and success; they are unwilling to pay the price of change.**

These people may get paid for 40 hours of work each week, yet actually give their employer maybe 32 hours of fruitful labor. By priding themselves on the ability to work as little as possible and still keep their jobs, they unknowingly *create* a life of mediocrity.

Even among individuals who say they want to be promoted, few ever survive the process of promotion. Promotion does not come by "coasting," or by just showing up at work every day. Promotion comes by turning up the heat and daily re-posturing yourself in order to go to a new level. Ask yourself: Am I an "excusiologist?"

George Washington Carver said, *"Ninety-nine percent of failures come from people who have a habit of making excuses."*

> BLAMING OTHERS
> IS PROOF THAT
> ONE HAS YET TO
> EMBRACE PERSONAL
> RESPONSIBILITY.

I call these people "excusiologists." That's a term I coined to define the many individuals I've observed through the years who look to blame others for their shortcomings. **Blaming others is proof one has yet to embrace personal responsibility.**

The excusiologist lives by these categorical lies:

- *"The reason I'm not succeeding is because other people don't want to help or involve me."*
- *"My boss won't promote me until I get more education, but he's not willing to pay for it."*
- *"Others have determined my future for me. I am a failure based on someone else's actions."*

So take a moment to ask yourself: *"Am I a person who makes excuses? Do I blame others for my lack of success in my business or career, in my home, or in my relationships?"*

There is a difference between an excuse and a justifiable reason. An excuse is merely an avoidance of responsibility. When you make excuses for something you have or have not done, you in actuality admit wrongdoing. In essence, you say, "I really should have worked it out another way, but I didn't. So here is my excuse for not doing it right."

Be careful not to make the poor decision to live your life the way much of today's world does — by making excuse after excuse. It is like rowing a boat that is tied to the dock. It doesn't produce anything but wasted energy. Don't say things such as, "If only this would have happened, things would have been different in my life." Going through each day as an excusiologist not only results in unfulfilled dreams, but also produces a negative attitude toward life.

Life is a series of *choices*, not a series of *chances*. Therefore, this is an important principle by which to live: **You change your life by changing your choices.**

But how does one begin to change his or her choices? I believe it is largely determined by one's outlook or perspective on life. The way you think about yourself and the world in which you live is critical to your success. One of the greatest truths ever written was penned by King Solomon. He stated, *"For as he thinks in his heart, so is he…"*

It doesn't matter if other people see you as a success; the question is, how do you see yourself? You will never obtain success in your business or place of employment until you see yourself as a success. Richard Bach confirmed this when he said, *"Sooner or later, those who win are those that think they can."*

Most people attain a certain level of success out of their fear of failure. Most people are so afraid of poverty that it drives them to riches. They work their fingers to the bone, save every penny they can, and never enjoy the fruits of their labor along the way. Others have learned how to enjoy life at another's expense, never learning how to pay for it themselves.

How about you? Take a few minutes and ask yourself these vital questions:

- *How serious am I about going to another level in the workplace, or even in life for that matter?*
- *Am I prepared to stop making excuses?*
- *Am I ready to stop seeing my place of employment as merely a "job," and start looking at it as a <u>position of purpose</u>?*
- *Am I going to invest in my goals by deciding to do whatever it takes to attain my highest level of performance at work?*
- *What am I prepared to do in order to get where I want to go in my career?*
- *How strong is my desire for success?*

Robert Collier once said: *"Plant the seed of desire in your mind, and it forms a nucleus with power to attract to itself everything needed for its fulfillment."* How true that is! I came to a crossroads in my life when I began to understand that: **I cannot fail without my consent, and I cannot succeed without my participation.**

If you desire a higher level of success in life, make a point to take ownership of your past. Don't buy into the lie that you are a victim and everyone is out to make you fail. If you fail, it is of your own consent. On the contrary, if you succeed, it is in part because you were willing to participate in your success.

> YOU CANNOT FAIL WITHOUT YOUR CONSENT, AND YOU CANNNOT SUCCEED WITHOUT YOUR PARTICIPATION.

You see, if anyone is ever going to move to higher levels of achievement at work, accepting personal responsibility is critical. We must choose *the hard way* and *do something different* until the new eclipses the old. The old doesn't just suddenly disappear, never to show up again. New thoughts produce a new paradigm, which will in turn produce a new life — a new way of doing things. Our new paradigm will begin to eclipse our old ways of thinking and acting. Finally, we become more motivated by success and integrity than by those old attitudes and habits that kept us in low-level living for so long.

It is this overriding hunger to pursue *personal virtue and excellence* that propels you upward to the next level. Remember: **Improvement is guaranteed only to those who are willing to change.**

> IMPROVEMENT IS
> GUARANTEED ONLY
> TO THOSE WHO ARE
> WILLING TO CHANGE.

Are you willing to sacrifice what you already have in order to possess what you truly value? Dreams only come true for those who are willing to give up their present in order to gain their future. What you are today is just a small taste of what you can be tomorrow. T. S. Eliot once said, *"Only those who will risk going too far can possibly find out how far one can go."*

Only a few determined individuals will set aside self-will and choose the difficult way of change and growth. As for me, I decided long ago to always choose the seemingly more difficult *but honorable way*, as I pursue the purposes and plans for my life. I don't ever choose the easy more convenient way, because I realize the easy way is ultimately unfruitful and often dishonorable, and usually requires a greater investment of my time in the long run.

So how do you start rising to the next level within the realm of your chosen occupation? How do you get from where you are now to the place where you are fulfilling your highest potential? (**Note:** These foundational principles of excellence apply to every area of your life.)

Let's discuss four principle ways to see success increase in your career.

1. Uphold Truth At All Costs

The first step toward real increase is to *have an unswerving dedication to truth*. Significant and lasting success is experienced by those who build their lives upon the firm foundation of truth.

No matter what I do, I always look for what it will take for me to receive a promotion. Through what gate do I need to pass to bring increase into my life? Ten years from now, I don't want to ask my mentors, "What do you think I did wrong these past ten years that kept me from the promotion I desired?" I want them to tell me right now what I need to do, so I can do it right the first time.

> THE EXCEPTIONAL LEARN FROM OTHERS' MISTAKES; WHILE THE FOOLISH DON'T EVEN LEARN FROM THEIR OWN.

I don't want to go through life like a ball in a pinball machine, bouncing from one side to another, trying to figure out what I should do to get to the next level in life. If I am able to discover through the wisdom of others what I need to do to be promoted, I can get rid of everything in my life that runs contrary to that wisdom. It is true that: **The exceptional learn from others' mistakes; while the foolish don't even learn from their own.**

Learn from the *wisdom of others*. Seek out a mentor who can adequately help you succeed. Put yourself on an accelerated course by accessing the wisdom of those who have been where you long to go. Learning from our own mistakes is great, but if we can bypass the mistakes and learn from the lessons others have learned, we can speed up the promotion process.

Allow the *wisdom of others* to guide you, so you can circumvent avoidable mistakes in the future!

2. Make Sacrifices

Every great man first had to make great sacrifices. Successful people understand the important role sacrifice plays. Sacrifice is one of those things many people prefer to avoid. When they hear an appeal for sacrifice, they ignore it and hope someone else responds.

> SACRIFICE
> IS THE ROAD TRAVELED
> BY THOSE WHO CHOOSE
> THE "HIGHER LIFE."

Those who learn to make sacrifices ultimately will go to a higher level, not only in their jobs, but also in every area of their life. You may have already discovered that there is no easy path to success.

Successful men and women are in huge demand to speak to crowds about the experiences they went through to get where they are today. The two most common sought after subjects about which these dynamic individuals are asked to talk are *the sacrifices* they had to make in the early years and *their determination never to quit,* no matter what. What will you have your name written among the few who have achieved the success they desired? Will others ask you about all the sacrifices you had to make to get to where you are today? It is your choice!

> THE BRILLIANT
> RESPOND TO AUTHORITY
> NOT WITH QUESTIONS
> BUT WITH COMPLIANCE.

3. Be Compliant In Heart And Action

The third crucial requirement to go to the next level in the workplace is *compliance.*

I am not implying that you comply with someone who asks you to do something against your conscience, such as something illegal or immoral. Of course, you must preserve your integrity at all cost. But even then, you need not communicate your refusal with a disrespectful or judgmental attitude. Authority simply must know that if you would lie *for* them, you would eventually also lie *to* them — and you respectfully refuse to do either! *Your unquestioning compliance to the instructions of honorable authority is the key to open innumerable doors of favor and promotion for you.*

Someone might say, "Well, it's hard to always do what my employer asks, but I still want to be promoted." You simply can't have it both ways.

I've learned to respond with unquestioning compliance to my authorities. My only question is, "What else can I do for you?" I do not look for ways *not* to do what I am asked. I realize, **repeated instruction constitutes correction.**

I don't sit and wait to hear the same thing twice. I don't question my superior's instructions. As far as I'm concerned, once it's spoken, it's done. I do it, and I do it with a positive attitude.

Following an instruction is not an option to those in pursuit of promotion; it is a way of life. It is the fragrance that emanates from their life. When it comes to compliance in the workplace the motto we can all live by is this: "The answer is yes. Now what is the question?"

4. Take Action

The fourth important factor for success is *take immediate action*. It doesn't do any good to have *intentions of compliance* if we walk away and forget to turn those intentions into actions. Realize that: **Intentions can only produce a barren life while productivity constructs a prosperous life.**

> INTENTIONS CAN ONLY PRODUCE A BARREN LIFE WHILE PRODUCTIVITY CONSTRUCTS A PROSPEROUS LIFE.

Your employer is not interested in what you intend to do. He looks at the bottom line. What did you do? Did you complete the assignment? Did you do what he asked? Always present your completions to your employer, not your intentions. How many people do you know who want a promotion, even if though they don't perform up to par? I know more than I can count. They want to be rewarded for trying! They want promotion for doing what they are paid to do. That is not the way it works.

When you do more than you are paid to do, promotion will come up in conversation. But promotion only comes after you complete your assigned tasks. You can't be lazy and succeed at the same time.

Laziness will definitely get your boss's attention, but not the kind of attention you desire! Let me give you a quick profile of a lazy employee:

- "Kills" time by sitting around visiting, or doing nothing.
- Continually watches the clock, anticipating the next break or the end of the day.
- Regularly looks for ways to delay work or avoid it altogether.
- Is irresponsible, and then expects others to pick up the slack.
- Acts "put out" and irritated when asked to increase efficiency or workload.
- Becomes an expert at looking busy, yet accomplishes nothing.
- Moves to a new project before completing the last one.
- Blames others for incomplete work.
- Is unwilling to pay the price to get to the next level.
- Puts more thought into vacations than into the future.
- Has many dreams and desires, but never sees them fulfilled.

If you saw yourself in any area as you went through the above check-list, I encourage you to shake off that "just-good-enough" attitude and focus on turning your intentions into completions. I discovered that: **the biggest difference between mediocrity and excellence is completion.**

Now, you probably can foresee already that this isn't as easy as it may sound. People talk about pursuing excellence all the time, but truly there are only a handful of individuals who accomplish it. I am not interested in just talking about or hearing about excellence — I want to *do* it and see it expressed in those around me. I'm determined to keep on pressing forward!

That's the stance you must take in order to be a person of excellence. You can't expect to live your life from a place of comfort and still

> PROMOTION STEMS
> FROM ACTIONS,
> WHILE FRUSTRATION
> IS THE RESULT
> OF INTENTIONS.

achieve success. Be okay with stretching yourself beyond your comfort zone — continue to go above and beyond in every area of your life, whether it's your personal accomplishments, your giving, or your role in the workplace.

To see the rewards of life come your way, you can't just talk about your goals. Your goals must turn into action.

Most people never get to the point where they turn their words into actions. They deceive themselves by *saying* they have great dreams and goals without ever *doing* anything to make those dreams come true. We can't just sit around and *think* about what we want to accomplish with our lives. Get honest with yourself, and take *action*.

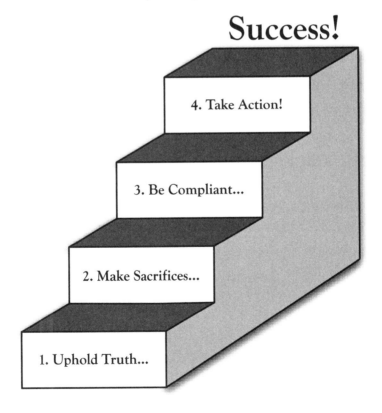

Success!

4. Take Action!

3. Be Compliant...

2. Make Sacrifices...

1. Uphold Truth...

THE STEP-BY-STEP CLIMB

A person does not move to a higher level of success in one huge leap. It is a step-by-step process. **See yourself at the level of success for which you aim long before you ever attempt to go there.**

That's the way I approached the issue of expanding our organization several years ago. For an entire year, I shut down everything and did not expand, because I was unsure of myself. I was unsure about who I was, where I was, and whether or not I had enough inner maturity and strength to successfully go on to the next level of multiplication that was being placed before me.

I believe that we always must make sure we have enough of what it takes to achieve success at the next level before launching out into it. I would go so far as to advise you to *turn away a promotion* if you don't *see* yourself functioning at that capacity. Many employees are eager to pursue promotion even when they are not truly ready for one.

HIGHER LEVELS REQUIRE HIGHER EXPERTISE

Someone once said to me, "You know, I love what I do for a living, but I just can't figure out the business end of it. What should I do?"

"I can tell you what I would do," I replied. "I'd sign up for a course on how to run a small business."

"But taking that course costs about two thousand dollars!" he responded.

"Yes," I countered. "But consider how much you're going to lose if you don't take a course like that, to give you the knowledge you need to be successful in business."

> THERE IS
> NO SUCH THING
> AS A SHORTCUT
> TO A BETTER LIFE.

If you are going to be successful, always keep learning. You simply cannot advance in any area of life without accurate and up-to-date knowledge. Once you begin to move up this ladder, be careful not to allow yourself to take a step backwards. Make the decision, "As long as I live, I will never live for short-term gratification. I'll keep my eyes focused on my goal — to live in excellence in the workplace and in every other area of my life!" That one decision will keep you from making a lot of unwise, unnecessary mistakes! **There is no such thing as a shortcut to a better life.**

We all must decide if we are willing to pay the price to succeed. Although sacrifice is a requirement to pursue the next level, refuse to shy away from paying the price. If you do, you have nothing to look forward to but a future filled with regret and disappointment!

CHAPTER ONE SUMMARY

- Life was designed to be a continual ascension. Excellence is, by its very definition, *progressive*. You cannot expect your level of excellence today to continue over until tomorrow. In order to excel, you must be willing to change for the better.

- Don't live your life the way much of today's world does — by making excuse after excuse. It is like rowing a boat that is tied to the dock. It doesn't produce anything but wasted energy.

- It doesn't matter if other people see you as a success; the question is, how do you see yourself? You will never obtain success in your business or place of employment until *you* see yourself as a success. Richard Bach confirmed this when he said, *"Sooner or later, those who win are those that think they can."*

- If you desire a higher level of success in life, you must first take ownership of your past. You must stop believing the lie that you are a victim and everyone is out to make you fail. If you fail, it is of your own consent. If you succeed, it is only because you were willing to participate in your success.

- The first step toward real increase is to *have an unswerving dedication to truth*. Significant and lasting success is experienced by those who build their lives upon the firm foundation of truth.

- *Be willing to make sacrifices.* A wise person is one who understands the importance of sacrifice. Sacrifice is one of those things many people prefer to avoid.

- The third crucial requirement for going to the next level in the workplace is *compliance*. The prophet Isaiah said, *"If you are willing and obedient, you will eat the best from the land."*

- The fourth important factor for success is *take immediate action*. It doesn't do any good to have *intentions of compliance* if we walk away and forget to turn those intentions into *actions*.

- Make the decision, "As long as I live, I will never live for short-term gratification. I'll keep my eyes focused on my goal — to live in excellence in the workplace and in every other area of my life!" This one decision will keep you from making a lot of stupid, unnecessary mistakes!

PRINCIPLES FOR DETERMINATION

→ Today's Excellence Is Tomorrow's Mediocrity.

→ Blaming Others Is Proof One Has Yet To Embrace Personal Responsibility.

→ On The List Of Things You Must Never Become, An "Excusiologist" Rates Number 1.

→ Change Is The Result Of Choices Not Chances.

→ You Cannot Fail Without Your Consent, And You Cannot Succeed Without Your Participation.

→ Improvement Is Guaranteed Only To Those Who Are Willing To Change.

→ The Exceptional Learn From Others' Mistakes; While The Foolish Don't Even Learn From Their Own.

→ Sacrifice Is The Road Traveled By Those Who Choose The "Higher Life."

→ Repeated Instruction Constitutes Correction.

→ Intentions Can Only Produce A Barren Life While Productivity Constructs A Prosperous Life.

→ The Biggest Difference Between Mediocrity And Excellence Is Finishing.

→ Promotion Stems From Actions, While Frustration Is The Result Of Intentions.

→ See Yourself At The Level Of Success For Which You're Aiming Long Before You Ever Attempt To Go There.

→ There Is No Such Thing As A Shortcut To A Better Life.

Focus:
The Key To Success

An inability to focus is the primary culprit that keeps us all from experiencing the change we desire. It is only through *focused movement toward your goal* that you attain the results you desire.

The first thing we must consider when talking about focus is that goals do not get accomplished *simply because we want them to*. On the contrary, **the proof of your desire is expressed by the intensity of your pursuit.**

You won't obtain your goal of advancement at your job by just talking about it. If you don't pursue it, you won't possess what you want. Desire is simply the first step, as spoken about by Samuel Smiles, "*An intense anticipation transforms possibility into reality; our desires being often but precursors of the things which we are capable of performing.*"

> THE PROOF
> OF YOUR DESIRE IS
> EXPRESSED BY
> THE INTENSITY
> OF YOUR PURSUIT.

In other words, *you have to maintain your focus!*

> TO ACHIEVE YOUR GOALS,
> CONTINUAL PURSUIT IS
> A NON-NEGOTIABLE.

Your words are the first indicator of the object of your focus. What comes out of your mouth is extremely important to steer your life in the right direction, much like the rudder of a ship. **Negative words are lethal enemies to positive goals.**

For instance, we can never cause someone to draw closer to us if we continually criticize that person. Likewise, we cannot receive promotions at our place of employment if we continually talk to the other employees about how terrible it is to work there. Your life will go in the direction of the words you speak. In both of these cases, words and actions point your life in the *opposite direction of your desired objective outcome*.

Focus also requires the elimination of options. An old adage says: "If you chase two rabbits, both will escape." There may be many good choices, but there is only one *best* choice. This is why people live confused not knowing exactly what decision they need to make. Therefore eliminating any unnecessary distractions from your life is important. Your success in any venture is dependent on what you are willing *to ignore*. The American business executive and millionaire, J. Paul Getty, once said, *"I've seen as many people fail in attempting to do too much, as too little."*

Consider the ancient story of Israel's powerful king, David. David was a man who was extremely confident in his ability to reign as king, and rightly so, for he had an impeccable track record. As king, David went out to war in the spring, just as all the other kings in the region did.

But one particular spring, he chose to stay home. He quit pursuing the very thing he was supposed to pursue. His focus waned and he became *distracted*. Laying down his sword and his shield, David started wondering what to do with all the time he had on his hands. He eventually found his answer — in the arms of another man's wife. It was a mistake that irrevocably altered the course of his future.

We all face the same dangers and temptations. **The most treacherous time we ever face in our lives is when things are going well.** That is when we start thinking, *"I need a break. I need to take a little more time off for fun than I've been doing."* We begin to take more vacations yet neglect the more important things to our life. Little by little, our broken focus starts us sliding down a slippery slope, into the abyss of mediocrity that has swallowed so many others before us.

> THE PRIMARY REASON
> FOR FAILURE IS
> BROKEN FOCUS.

Broken focus is all too common in our self-indulgent society. When people first recognize and identify their dreams and goals, they pursue them with fervor. They go after it! They start off well, full of enthusiasm, and are extremely diligent. But then, little by little, they get distracted and start pursuing other things. Soon they go through each day feeling out of control and disappointed. Why? Because their focus has been tainted and they slowly stop pursuing their dreams. They don't realize that, **follow-through and finishing are the only doors to promotion.**

What are you hired to do? When you focus, often the only person who recognizes it is the person you seek to please. When your employer recognizes that your motives are pure and you focus on completing the tasks he has assigned to you, he will allow you to make more decisions on your own.

Pleasing others is a somewhat interesting issue. When I speak about being pleasing to others, people often have reservations. They are unsure that they won't be controlled. But to be quite honest, I have yet to see anyone be controlled whose desire is to please. You can't control those who *want* to be pleasing.

Therefore, it is important to know that every significant relationship includes someone that we are supposed to please. When I know who that person is, I focus on bringing pleasure to that person's life. I constantly ask myself: *What can I do for him that will please him? How can I help make life easier for him?*

> FOCUS ON WHAT YOU
> WANT, OR SETTLE FOR
> WHAT YOU GET.

I understand that in relationships and in every issue of life, to truly succeed, I must focus on what I want, or settle for what I get.

I have experienced first hand how the power of focus can change a person's destiny. There was a time, back in 1975, when my *whole life needed to be re-focused.* For years my life was a wreck. Eventually, I began to lose my mind and ended up in a mental institution. But then came a day when my life completely changed. I discovered the necessity of embracing spiritual peace and balance; I bowed my knee and cried out to God for help. Over night my life was radically transformed.

Now, inasmuch as I am thankful to God for my life, the responsibility to change was mine. **I had to refocus my life and assess what truly mattered most. My focus changed and as a result my life was transformed.**

THE POWER OF FOCUSED THOUGHTS

The very first arena that needed to change back in 1975 was *the way that I thought.* My reckless life was the result of insolvent and destructive thinking. I soon realized that my life was an outer projection of my inner image. **If my life was going to be different, I had to change the way I thought.**

Perhaps you are familiar with the kind of thought patterns I am speaking about. Do you approach a problem with an attitude saying, "Oh, no, not again! Everything always goes wrong in my life! Everything is just so horrible. Every day I get up just to get knocked down all over again!"?

The thoughts you allow to dock at the harbor of your mind determine the attitude you express. Do you perceive life from the perspective that your cup is half empty or your cup is half full? Do you look at life from the viewpoint

> **THE PROBLEM KNOCKING AT YOUR DOOR IS YOUR GREATEST OPPORTUNITY FOR SURE.**

that says, "Look how far I still have to go" or "Look how far I've come"? Do you perceive obstacles to be the emissary of defeat in your life, or the springboard to a higher level of victory?

Sir Winston Churchill said these words, *"The pessimist sees difficulty in every opportunity. The optimist sees the opportunity in every difficulty."* How true that is! I like to say it like this: **The problem knocking at your door is your greatest *opportunity for sure.***

We will all experience setbacks at some point in our lives. We will be disappointed with others and life won't play out just as we planned. We must prepare for and welcome the day that we encounter these setbacks and disappointments. Obstacles and setbacks are necessary for promotion. In fact, every problem or adverse circumstance is only a promotion in disguise waiting to be discovered. The circumstances of life are what you must overcome to become a champion.

I am reminded of David again. He fearlessly withstood the giant warrior, Goliath. What inspired this shepherd lad? What caused him to do what no other soldier was willing to do? What inspired David to fight? Simply put, *reward.* David never ran at Goliath until he heard of the generous reward of the king. Like David, when you focus on the reward, you'll run *toward* your Goliath to defeat him. If you focus on the size of your giant, you'll run *away* from him. It's all in what you allow yourself to focus on and imagine. What you focus on will enlarge. Therefore you must keep your focus on the reward.

Ask yourself, *"How do I view my situation? Do I focus on the problem or the solution? Do I look at it with the attitude that I can overcome my giant, or do I expect him to pound me into the ground? Have I learned from my past mistakes, or have I allowed one mistake to be my undoing?"*

Henry Ford, the creator of the first automobile, observed, *"A mistake may turn out to be the one thing necessary to a worthwhile achievement."*

Re-assess and re-focus your thinking. Take inventory of what you have been focusing on. Learn to perceive every problem as a possibility, every loss as a clearer revelation on how to win, and every battleground as an *opportunity to pass a test* and be promoted to a higher level. **Run towards the roar of your enemy, saying, "I won't quit! I won't give in to negativity! I will not throw in the towel! I will continue to hang in there, and I will be a winner!"**

THE CUP OF LIFE

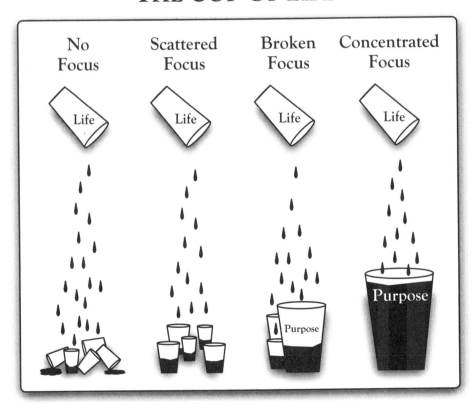

THE POWER OF FOCUSED GENEROSITY

The second arena of my life that I drastically re-focused was the arena of my giving. I discovered that a lifestyle of generosity was *required* in order for me to go to another level of success in my work and in my life.

Generosity is anything of value to you that you happily give to another. It can be money, time, talents, gifts, respect, a helping hand, and so forth. The philosophy behind this principle is that when you give as the way you would plant a seed, it multiplies and produces a harvest for you.

> THOSE WHO WILL BE WISE UNDERSTAND THE POWER OF GENEROSITY.

Your generosity transports you from where you are to where you need to go. This is a very powerful principle that many of the wealthiest people and most successful corporations have embraced.

When people can't seem to break through in the arena of their finances, it is often because they have never reached a level of *focused, sacrificial* giving. Instead, they live in the realm of *indiscriminate, convenience* giving: "Let's give a little something to these poor people — they need it." Many people you know have a scarcity mindset. They tend to hold on to what they have, especially when it comes to their money. Because if they let go, they are uncertain it will come back into their life. **The law of sowing and reaping guarantees that whatever you sow comes back to you in multiplied fashion.** Your part is to let go and walk in a greater level of generosity than ever before.

The more you give, the easier it becomes; however, until you practice, it may just be the hardest thing you've ever done. Focus on one thing as you give — you *will* reap in due season if you remain diligent.

SEE BEYOND YOUR FEARS

The presence of fear is proof that focus has been placed on the wrong object or outcome of your situation or circumstances. Take captive the fearful thoughts that attempt to cripple you. You become whatever thoughts you dwell upon. Deal severely with fearful thoughts, as if they are threatening your very life. Throw them out and replace them with thoughts of belief, faith, and success.

> FEAR IS THE JAILER THAT VOWS TO KEEP YOU FROM SUCCESS.

Success is no more than the willingness to bear pain, therefore face your fears and act regardless of their silent roars. How many songs have gone unwritten because of fear? How many speeches have gone unspoken because of this deadly enemy? How many dreams have breathed their last because of fear? President Franklin D. Roosevelt said, *"The only limit to our realization of tomorrow will be our fears of today."*

Fear paralyzes. It disrupts our ability to make decisions. It undermines our resolution for success. If left unchecked, it rusts the gears of life and ultimately results in ruin. You must counter-attack fear. Face your fears and watch them fade away right before your eyes.

During the worst years of the Great Depression, President Franklin D. Roosevelt told the American people, *"The only thing to fear is fear itself."*

Arthur Wellesley, the Duke of Wellington, once said, *"The only thing I am afraid of is fear."*

Francis Bacon is quoted as saying, *"Nothing is terrible except fear itself."*

It seems as though throughout history, great achievers came to the same conclusion: **it is not our circumstances that threaten to destroy us—it is our fear of them.**

Fear paralyzes you. It disrupts your ability to trust your decisions, and therefore robs you of your resolve to succeed. Fear, if left unchecked, stops your progress and ultimately destroys your life.

The noted Franklin D. Roosevelt penned these words, *"The only limit to our realization of tomorrow will be our doubts of today."*

FOCUS ON THE VISION

A well-known proverb states, *"Where there is no vision, the people perish..."* In other words, when you lose focus, you open the door to destruction. That's why it is so important to remove from your life the hindrances that cause you to lose your focus. In most cases if you want to walk in a higher level of excellence and attain the promotion you desire, this principle is vital: **The excellent view life through the eyes of unbroken focus.**

> EXCELLENCE VIEWS LIFE THROUGH THE EYES OF UNBROKEN FOCUS.

Too many individuals go backward instead of forward in life. There are two reasons for this. First, they never clearly define their vision. Or second, they no longer keep the vision before their eyes. Most people simply exist hoping everything they want will somehow appear in their life. And truthfully, **accelerated growth can only be achieved by pursuit of what you desire.**

Defining your vision is something that requires an internal evaluation, asking the questions that cause you to look into your soul. Taking the time to do so will cause clarity to come into your life. The law of clarity says, the clearer you are about where you want to go, the quicker you can get there. Be clear about what you want and pursue it at all costs.

> ACCELERATED GROWTH CAN ONLY BE ACHIEVED BY PURSUIT OF WHAT YOU DESIRE.

If you desire your vision to become larger, then keep it before your eyes. Write it down. Have a dream wall where you put pictures of what you want. Somehow find a way to keep the vision for your life before you at all times. Focus causes anything to grow. Therefore focus on your vision and it will grow on the inside of you. Soon it will become too large for your present environment to contain what's inside you.

Success, personal growth, and promotion don't come because you want them. They come because you deserve them. You work hard for them and they will come into your life. But not only do you have to work for them, you also must see yourself walking in them, before you ever really do. **Because your life will always move in the direction of your most dominant thoughts.**

RE-SET YOUR FOCUS

Too often, people take their eyes off their goals and dreams. Maybe they are excited about their future for a while, but then things change.

Everyone starts pulling at them from all different directions—at work and at home—wanting them to take on greater responsibilities.

So it goes, day after day. At the end of each day, they promise themselves that tomorrow will be different — "Tomorrow I'll pursue my dream." Then the next day, they say, "Oh, I have too much to do today. I'll have to go after this goal tomorrow."

If that sounds familiar, the solution to your problem is simple. Just re-set your focus. Get your eyes back on your long-term dreams and goals. Decide to give your attention to what is important rather than what is urgent. Take the time to re-focus and always put your vision before your eyes. Write it down! Imagine it! Speak it! And live it out! **Let the power of focus resurrect the purpose of your life!**

CHAPTER TWO SUMMARY

- An inability to focus is the primary culprit that keeps us from experiencing the changes for which we so greatly long in our lives. It is only through *focused movement toward your goal* that you attain the results you desire.

- *You only possess what you are willing to pursue.* You won't obtain your goal of advancement at your job by just talking about it. If you don't pursue it, you won't possess it.

- The most treacherous time we ever face in our lives is when things are going well. That is when we start thinking, "*I need a break. I need to take a little more time off for fun than I've been doing.*"

- The very first arena that needed a complete change of focus when this transformation came to my life was *the way that I thought*. My destitute life had been the result of destitute and destructive thinking. If my life was going to be different, my thinking had to be different.

- You must prepare for and welcome the day that you encounter obstacles of any sort. Obstacles and setbacks are necessary for promotion. The circumstances of life are what you must overcome to become a champion.

- The second arena of my life that I drastically re-focused was the arena of my giving. I discovered that a lifestyle of generosity was *required* in order for me to go to another level of success in my work and in my life.

- The presence of fear is proof that focus has been placed on the wrong object or outcome of your situation or circumstances. You must discipline yourself to take captive the fearful thoughts that attempt to cripple you. You will become whatever you allow yourself to dwell upon.

• During the worst years of the Great Depression, President Franklin D. Roosevelt told the American people, *"The only thing to fear is fear itself."*

• Arthur Wellesley, the Duke of Wellington, once said, *"The only thing I am afraid of is fear."*

• Francis Bacon is quoted as saying, *"Nothing is terrible except fear itself."*

• Get your eyes back on your *long-term* dreams and goals. Decide to give your attention to what is *important* rather than what is *urgent*. Take the time to re-focus and always put your vision before your eyes. Write it down! Imagine it! Speak it! And live it out!

PRINCIPLES FOR FOCUS

→ Broken Dreams Are The Result Of Broken Focus.

→ The Proof Of Your Desire Is Expressed By The Intensity Of Your Pursuit.

→ To Achieve Your Goals, Continual Pursuit Is A Non-Negotiable.

→ The Primary Reason For Failure Is Broken Focus.

→ Follow Through And Completion Are The Biggest Doors To Promotion.

→ Focus On What You Want, Or Settle For What You Get.

→ The Rewards Of Life Arrive Only Upon The Doorstep Of The Overcomer.

→ Those Who Will Be Wise Understand The Power Of The Seed.

→ Your Seed Is The Greatest Tool To Achieve A Transformed Life.

→ Your Seed Of Today Creates The Harvest Of Tomorrow.

→ Fear Is The Jailer That Vows To Keep You From Success.

→ Accelerated Growth Can Only Be Achieved By Pursuit Of What You Desire.

→ Excellence Views Life Through The Eyes Of Unbroken Focus.

Goals:
Multiplying
Your Life Investment

TO SUCCEED,
YOU MUST CONTINUALLY POINT
YOUR LIFE IN THE DIRECTION OF
YOUR DESIRED DESTINATION.

You probably wouldn't be reading this book if you didn't have a desire to move upward in your profession. But you need to know more than just what steps to take in order to reach the next level. You also need to learn how to multiply what you've been given in life, so you can accelerate your personal growth, which in turn accelerates your progress in the workplace.

You were born with a need to grow. That's why, when you first start a new job, you come in with such high hopes of advancement and promotion. You were created to multiply the gifts that were placed inside of you, and to be happy, fulfilled, and successful.

Establishing Life Purpose

Your first step toward multiplying your life investment is to discover your life purpose. If you don't understand what you're supposed to do with your life, you and those around you abuse it. Take a knife for example. It can either be used to cut meat or another individual. If you know the purpose of a knife, you won't misuse it.

> An Abused Life Is Simply A Life Without Purpose.

It is my personal desire never to waste or squander a moment of this life that God has graciously given to me. I want to invest my life in ways that will give the greatest benefit to my loved ones and future generations. If that is your desire as well, let's review the questions you need to answer as you set out on your life course:

- *Where do I want to go in life?*
- *What is my life assignment?*
- *What do I want to achieve in the days and years to come?*
- *What am I currently doing toward the fulfillment of my goals?*

King Solomon said, *"The soul of a lazy man desires, and has nothing; but the soul of the diligent shall be made rich."* Most people spend their entire lives desiring what they do not have, yet at the same time they are unwilling to prepare themselves *today* in order to achieve *tomorrow*. These same people usually find a way to blame others for their inability to get what they want. But you can never rightfully blame others for your own lack of success. **You are responsible for the outcome of your life. No one else is. Not those in your past, not those who are close to you today, no one is responsible, but you.**

The willingness to accept responsibility causes you to really think about what life is all about. It causes you to ask questions such as: where am I going in life? What do I want to accomplish? When I write about responsibility, I am reminded about the famous quote of William P. Merrill, *"Unless you give yourself to some great cause, you haven't even begun to live."* The reason why most individuals never achieve a high level of success is that they never set any goals for themselves.

They don't know where they are going in life nor how they are going to get there. In reality they just exist day after day, thinking, *"Maybe someone will discover how great I am one of these days!"* But I can tell you right now, no one ever will.

High achievers are those individuals who decide to make a difference in this world. They are determined to leave a mark on society that would not have been there if they had not been born. These are the kinds of people Benjamin Disraeli referred to when he said, *"Nothing can resist the human will that will stake even its existence on its stated purpose."*

The life we live is coming to a close one day. Statistically, ten out of ten people die. With every breath we take, we are one breath closer to the end. I am not going to wait until I'm old and sitting in my rocking chair to tell my grandchildren that they need to pursue excellence, or that they need to be people who keep their word. I'm going to live my life at the highest level that I can right *now*, before those grandchildren are ever born, so I can speak into their lives from their earliest memories. If I'd have had someone to teach me these things when *I* was young, I would be much further than where I am today.

POINT YOUR LIFE IN THE RIGHT DIRECTION

So, how do you accelerate your progress in the workplace? The first thing you have to do is to take an inventory of your present skills, abilities, and areas of expertise. What you are *good* at? What skills or talents do you possess? What do you most like to do? On a scale of 1-10 where would you rate yourself?

Personally, one of the things that upsets me most is mediocrity. **It's not what you have but what you do with what you have that determines your success or failure.** Abraham Maslow, the great psychologist, said that the story of the human race is the story of people selling themselves short...people have a tendency to settle for far less from life than they are truly capable of. Many people spin their wheels in careers where they should be moving rapidly onward and upward.

When I see a person doing nothing with his life, it makes me angry! I think, "Man, you're just taking up precious air! Someone else could take your place and do something with his life!"

Excellence is my passion. My aspiration is to eradicate mediocrity and instill an unending desire for excellence in the life of every person with whom I come in contact. In the same way, you need to discover your life mission and then point your life in that direction.

GET RID OF THE EXTRA WEIGHTS

Your life cannot launch off the proverbial pad to the next level unless you rid yourself of the extra weights that hold you down. We all have areas of our character and our thought life that need improvement. In order to see continual success we must pursue constant growth! **Growth always occurs on the inside before it ever manifests on the outside.**

Attempting to change one's self from the outside might appear to work in the short term, but it is only a temporary change. Most of the problems with which you deal do not stem from an outside source. *Your main problem is internal* — in your own mind. Change begins in the mind. Unless you change your thoughts, you cannot alter your life.

A man's life is a reflection of his inward *thoughts*. If you desire to change your life, you must begin by changing the way that you think. Let me say it like this, **in order to transform your life, you must be willing to change your mind.**

> IN ORDER TO TRANSFORM YOUR LIFE, YOU MUST BE WILLING TO CHANGE YOUR MIND.

We all have thoughts that hold us back. More than likely, you have self-limiting beliefs that keep you from moving forward. It may be thoughts such as, "I'll never get that promotion," or "My boss hates me," or "I'm not a good employee." I encourage you throughout your day to take an inventory of your thoughts. Jot them down and counteract them with a new thought that is uplifting...one that will move you closer to your desired destination. You *must* shed the thoughts that hinder you before they ultimately destroy your life.

I recommend that you take the time to evaluate your thoughts. What is your self-talk? What do you say to yourself on a daily basis? Do these thoughts harm your effectiveness to fulfill your life's purpose? If so, you need to eliminate that hindrance from your life. Your thoughts truly do matter. What you believe about yourself makes a difference. **Your thoughts become actions that determine the outcome of your life.** Therefore it is important for you to take rein over your thoughts in order to take control over your life.

YOUR TIME = YOUR LIFE

Go after what you want, but realize this, you can't do everything. You only have twenty-four hours in a day. Every minute takes you either closer to or further from your intended destiny. Therefore, you need to ask yourself, *"What's the most valuable use of my time?"*

Your top priority should be to accomplish the purpose for which you were born. Everything in your life must revolve around this goal, and that includes your present vocation.

> ALL OF US HAVE TWENTY-FOUR HOURS EACH DAY. THE ONLY DIFFERENCE BETWEEN ANY OF US IS HOW WE SPEND THEM.

I have learned that I can no longer just *do what I want to do* — instead, *I do what I **must** do.* Only those who want to live in mediocrity "do what they want."

Unless you can manage your time and use it to invest into your future, you will not succeed. If you do not use the twenty-four hours you have to invest into your future, you will not attain the promotion you desire.

Identify and eliminate any habit, relationship, interest, or activity that hinders you from pursuing your life assignment. If you are going to *multiply* what has been invested into you, you can't hold on to anything

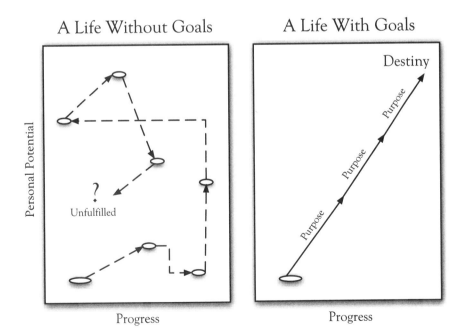

A Life Without Goals

A Life With Goals

Personal Potential

Progress

Unfulfilled

?

Destiny

Purpose

Purpose

Purpose

Progress

that subtracts or divides! What eats up your time? What hinders you from moving towards promotion? What books can you read to show you how to succeed? Benjamin Franklin said it like this, *"Waste your time and waste your life for that is what life is made of."*

CONTINUALLY STRIVE TO EXCEL

Ask yourself this question in order to receive the greatest return on your life investment: *Do I continue to excel toward my 100-percent potential?*

When this question becomes the measuring stick for your perform-ance in the workplace, people begin to say, "You know you are such a perfectionist." But whenever people tell me that, I just respond, "No, I'm not a perfectionist. I am a person of excellence — always pursuing becoming better, but knowing that it is a life-long pursuit."

You see, perfection is always beyond human reach, but excellence is something attainable — a standard you can move toward. **You can become better every day, in every area of your life! The question is, will you?**

I want to excel in what I've been given to do. Every day, I do my absolute best and do whatever is needed of me. I strive to make my best *even better.* That's how I operate every day of my life. I can never be perfect this side of Heaven, but I *can always* pursue excellence.

When you make the choice to continually strive to excel, some-thing changes on the inside of you. Perhaps you already have taken the necessary steps to reach the next level. You may even be the biggest and the best fish in your little pond. But do you know what normally happens when you reach that point? As you grow, you are soon moved to a much bigger pond, where once again you are the smallest fish! Why does this happen? So that you can grow to be an even bigger fish!

If you keep fish in a small aquarium, those fish stay small. But when you put those same fish into a larger aquarium, you give them the means to grow to greater potential.

> EXCELLENCE
> IS A JOURNEY,
> NOT A DESTINATION.
> IT IS A PROCESS,
> NOT AN EVENT.

That's what happens for you as well. You are given room to excel within your current level. Then you are promoted, so you can continue to grow in your gifts and talents.

Always keep this in mind: **Excellence is a journey, not a destination. It is a process, not an event.**

Excellence is an ongoing process, whereas perfection is a destination. As long as you strive to excel, you are on a continuous journey toward a promising future.

THE POWER OF A FINISHER

Are you a finisher or just a starter? Anyone can start a project — but only a few bring that project to completion. If you want to be a sought after individual in your place of employment, you need to master this important success principle: **Never seek another instruction until you successfully complete your last one.**

> NEVER SEEK
> ANOTHER INSTRUCTION
> UNTIL YOU HAVE
> SUCCESSFULLY COMPLETED
> YOUR LAST ONE.

Here's a question you may want to ask yourself in order to evaluate whether or not you are a finisher: *In my position at work, have I been faithful to the point of being approached by an expert in my field because he has recognized my desire for and pursuit of excellence?*

Leaders move toward the person who answers their most immediate challenges. This includes business owners and supervisors in the workplace. It also explains one of the main reasons a supervisor might go around someone and give an opportunity to the person who actually has a lower position than he does.

This situation usually develops because, at one time or another, that employee was asked to do something that he for some reason or another did not do. So the supervisor concludes that he cannot count on that employee, and he starts to gravitate instead to the one who will complete the assigned task. He will gravitate to the one who is the "go-to" person. That's the person who responds every time by saying, "I can do that, Sir. I'll take care of it." The "go-to" person doesn't just say he'll do it; *he actually does it.*

In order to be the person *your* employer gravitates toward when he needs something, adopt this principle: **A "go-to" person is defined by solving every problem to which they are assigned.**

> A "GO-TO" PERSON
> IS DEFINED BY
> SOLVING EVERY PROBLEM
> TO WHICH THEY
> ARE ASSIGNED.

Most people are tremendous starters, but very few finish well. They start with great expectations, but they just can't seem to bring what they start to completion. They talk a good talk; they sell themselves with their words. But, ultimately, they don't make it happen.

In the workplace, these people may be given the benefit of the doubt for a number of years. But eventually their true self will be found out. If you neglect to finish your assigned projects, soon enough you will receive less and less responsibilities.

If I had to choose one thing that frustrates me most it is when people do not fully follow through on what they said they would do. I have had international leaders tell me, "I'm going to take care of this. I'm going to help your organization in this way." So I spend time getting

> REFUSE TO MOVE
> FROM THE CENTER
> OF YOUR ASSIGNMENT
> UNTIL, AFTER THOROUGH
> EXAMINATION,
> YOU CAN SAY,
> "IT IS FINISHED."

myself into position for their words to come to pass — and then nothing happens. It was all a waste of time.

By contrast, I have a particular friend in my life that is not only a good starter, but a great finisher. He calls me and says things like, "I have scheduled you to speak at this conference, Robb. This person will be in contact with you concerning that engagement, and I'll talk to you next week to make sure everything has been taken care of." *Now that's an executor!*

If *you* want to be known as a faithful executor, make this your guiding principle: **Refuse to move from the center of your assignment until, after thorough examination, you can say, "It is finished."**

That's the way you build a reputation as a finisher. Stay persistent and focus on the completion of what you have been assigned to do. You will finish if you do not let up!

NEVER STOP MOVING FORWARD

One of the most dangerous positions to take in life is to remain stationary. You either move forward or backward at any given moment. At every moment you either multiply your life investment, or you squander it through neglect and disuse. **You either take steps toward your best performance, or you move backward toward mediocrity. There is no middle ground.**

The first thing that happens when you go backward is that you begin to go without. Then you start to think, "*I knew this would never work,*" and your wrong thoughts continue to take you further back. If you continue in that direction, your life ends up worse than it was when you first began your quest to fulfill your purpose in life.

Rid your mind of any negative thoughts such as, *"You'll never make it. You're no good. Things aren't going to work out for you. That kind of success is only possible for other people."*

Do whatever it takes to *press in*. No matter how small your step may be, just make sure you make forward progress. Don't take a step backward. Refuse to give up the progress you have already attained. **Nothing will be impossible as you persistently pursue the achievement of your goals.**

CHAPTER THREE SUMMARY

- Your first step toward multiplying your life investment is to discover your life purpose. If you don't understand what you're supposed to do with your life, you and those around you misuse it. Take a knife for example. It can either be used to cut meat or another person. If you know the purpose of something, you won't misuse it.

- A wise king once said, *"The soul of a lazy man desires, and has nothing; but the soul of the diligent shall be made rich."* Many people spend their entire lives desiring what they don't have. Yet they are unwilling to apply themselves *today* in order to prepare for *tomorrow.*

- High achievers are those individuals who have decided to make a difference in this world. They are going to leave a mark on society that would not have been there if they had not been born.

- So, how do you accelerate your growth in the workplace? The first thing you have to do is to take an inventory of your present skills, abilities, and areas of expertise.

- Your life cannot launch off the proverbial pad to the next level in life unless you rid yourself of the extra weights that hold you down. We all have areas of our character and our thought life that need improvement. In order to see continual success we must be pursue constant growth!

- We all have thoughts that hold us back. More than likely, you have self-limiting beliefs that keep you from moving forward. It may be thoughts such as, *"I'll never get that promotion,"* or *"My boss hates me,"* or *"I'm not a good employee."*

- Identify and eliminate any habit, relationship, interest, or activity that hinders you from pursuing your life assignment. If you are going to *multiply* what has been invested into you, you can't hold on to anything that subtracts or divides!

- When you continually strive to excel, something changes on the inside of you.

- Excellence is an ongoing process, whereas perfection is a specific point of arrival or attainment. As long as you strive to excel, you move in the direction of a promising future.

- You see, most people are tremendous starters, but very few finish well. They start with great expectations, but they just can't bring their goal to completion.

- You cannot be stationary in life. You either go forward or backward at any given moment. You either multiply your life investment, or you squander it through neglect and disuse.

- Rid your mind of any negative thoughts such as, *"You'll never make it. You're no good. Things aren't going to work out for you. That kind of success is only possible for other people."*

PRINCIPLES FOR GOALS

⇥ A Life Abused Is Simply A Life Without Purpose.

⇥ To Transform Your Life, You Must Be Willing To Change Your Mind.

⇥ All Of Us Have Twenty-Four Hours Each Day. The Only Difference Between Any Of Us Is How We Spend Them.

⇥ Excellence Is A *Journey*, Not A *Destination*. It Is A *Process*, Not An *Event*.

⇥ Never Seek Another Instruction Until You *Successfully Complete* Your Last One.

⇥ Leaders Move Toward The Person Who Answers Their Most Immediate Challenges.

⇥ A "Go-To" Person Is Defined By Solving Every Problem To Which They Are Assigned.

⇥ Refuse To Move From The Center Of Your Assignment Until, After Thorough Examination, You Can Say, "It Is Finished."

Respect:
The Prerequisite For Promotion

RESPECT IS MAGNETIC;
IT ATTRACTS WHAT YOU CRAVE,
WHILE DISRESPECT REPELS IT.

Respect is one of the qualities that bring great return on any investment in the workplace. For instance, if you do not understand or
respect your finances, money leaves you. You may earn a lot of money,
but you are never able to accumulate it. On the other hand, if you both
understand and respect the value of money, it comes toward you and
overtakes your life.

This is true in any arena of life, especially relationships. If you act
disrespectfully or indifferently toward a person, that person distances
himself from you and ultimately exits your life.

For example, in marriage, a spouse who isn't given respect may not
leave the marriage *physically*, but he or she certainly becomes emotion-
ally distant from the one who acts disrespectfully. On the other hand,
marriage partners who show respect to one another find themselves
drawing increasingly closer through the years. You see, *intimacy* doesn't
necessarily guarantee access to a person, but *respect does*.

THE MEANING OF "RESPECT"

Respect is a very interesting word. Society has spent the last forty years dismantling the meaning of the word *respect*. As a result, many people don't even know what this word means. They don't respect themselves, let alone someone else! Nonetheless, respect is a powerful force, absolutely essential to multiply your life investment within the workplace.

So let's talk about the meaning of the word *respect*. In part, it means *giving attention to*. Respect also carries the meaning of *holding others in high esteem or deeming others as distinguished and worthy*.

Think about it — who do you hold in high esteem? To whom do you give your attention? Who are the distinguished people in your life that you consider worthy of honor?

In your work situation, you need to give your honor and attention to all individuals but especially to those who are over you. I don't want my employees to give attention to what *other* employees or employers think about the dynamics of working in this establishment. What other people think about what goes on within the walls of our world head-quarters really does not matter to me. They have no authority over this organization because they are not responsible for it.

Often, the reason an employee views other employers as better than his own is that he doesn't have to submit to those other employers. The employee might say, "I just love the way that person runs his business," not realizing how difficult it would be to work under the tough standards of that particular employer.

Respect is a quality that lives on the inside of a person. The truth is, all of life is lived from the internal rather than from the external. In fact, I'll go so far as to say **the way a person lives on the outside is the way he is on the inside.**

All you need to do is look at the inside of your car if you want to find out how you're doing on the inside of *you*. If you have a mold farm growing on some five-month-old French fries stuck beneath the front seat, that's a good indication that you need to make some changes!

I know what I'm talking about because of the way I was raised. The unkempt condition of our home was only a reflection of the chaos and turmoil that lived on the inside of each member of my family.

As a young boy, I knew my mom was drinking if I opened the front door of our house and found myself suddenly ankle-deep in newspapers, dirt, and junk scattered all over the floor. If I ever wanted to find something to wear, I had to find it in the pile of clothes that always lay on the floor. Nothing was ever hung in a closet.

The disorder on the inside of my parents became the way our entire family lived on the outside. I'm so grateful that, years later, both my parents decided to pursue divine ethics and principles in their lives, and they were changed from the inside out!

Because respect is an inward quality, no one can make another into a respectful person. **A person is respectful because he chooses to be respectful.**

You see, people cannot earn respect. They may earn others' *adherence* or *false loyalty*, but they don't earn their *respect*. Respect is a quality originating in a person's mind, and a course of action that proceeds from that person's esteem for others. It involves giving due attention and showing respect to another.

RESPECT IN THE WORKPLACE

Respect of others makes a huge difference in the workplace, because *respect guarantees access*. A person who is respectful cannot be stopped, because respect is really nothing more than a seed. If it is sown into the lives of others, it brings a harvest of respect and favor back into the life of the one who sowed it. Respect will multiply your investments, while *disrespect is the thief that steals your promotion.*

An employer is almost always willing to listen to an employee who

> DISRESPECT
>
> IS THE THIEF THAT
>
> STEALS YOUR PROMOTIONS.

is respectful and conducts his affairs rightly. That's the kind of employee to whom an employer is willing to listen all day long!

Most of the time it is not just the quality of your work that gets you noticed on the job. **It is respect that gets a person promoted; thereafter, the quality of that person's work keeps him on that higher level.**

I personally know many individuals who work very hard but are disrespectful toward their boss. They wonder why the boss never seems to notice them when it comes time for promotion. I know exactly why they get bypassed. It is their disrespect that keeps them from being promoted.

Success follows respect. Learn to respect and you will attract to you the very things you desire. Promotion tends to overlook anyone who disrespects those in authority. Disrespect subverts rather than multiplies any investment a person has made at his job. Think about it. Can an employer put disrespect in a position of authority? Of course not! If he did, it would result in anarchy in the workplace.

Over the years, I have observed that disrespectful people have a tendency to be angry, afraid, or insecure.

First, they may be angry that no one has discovered their "worthiness" to be placed in a position of authority. They refuse to admit that they may not have been "discovered" yet because they're *not ready* to be discovered!

Second, a disrespectful person may be afraid that he will be taken advantage of if he yields to someone else's way of doing things. The root of this fear is a lack of trust. In other words, the person does not trust those who have been placed over him in authority.

A disrespectful person may also feel insecure because he is unsure of his position within the organization. He begins to perceive the decisions of his superiors as a threat to his own security. However, a person who knows his role has no issues with insecurity. He is a confident individual who has no problem showing respect to others knowing it will yield him a great return.

Disrespect in the workplace is a tragedy. It is the reason so many people come to a standstill in their vocation. No matter what level a person is in the workplace, respect is an absolute requirement for any future promotion.

In fact, there are two great proverbs that promise *great* rewards of multiplication and promotion to those who are respectful and pure of heart:

> *He who loves purity of heart and has grace on his lips, the king will be his friend.*
>
> *Do you see a man who excels in his work? He will stand before kings; he will not stand before unknown men.*

Grace on a person's lips brings royalty and favor to his friendships and surroundings. The person who excels at pureness of heart and consistently speaks respectful words of grace in the workplace will not remain in the background. He will continue to be promoted to positions of greater responsibility until one day he stands before men of influence. In other words, he finds supernatural favor with those in the highest positions of honor and authority!

WHAT PART DO I PLAY IN THIS RELATIONSHIP?

Many times your level of respect is dependent upon your ability to recognize who you are and more importantly who you are not in any given relationship. You have to be able to accurately answer the question, *"What part do I play in the relationship I have with this person?"* **A person of excellence assesses who and what he is in every relationship and then postures himself accordingly.**

> A PERSON OF EXCELLENCE ASSESSES WHO AND WHAT HE IS IN EVERY RELATIONSHIP AND THEN POSTURES HIMSELF ACCORDINGLY.

Whether or not a person recognizes who he is in his relationships determines the outcome of those relationships. For instance, as an employer, my staff members have to *respect the position of authority* in which I stand, even if they do not respect me as a person.

"Well, yes, but what happens if you do a poor job of exercising your authority?" I am not advocating poor ethics, but the point I am attempting to bring across is that our respect is not dependent upon the other person. It is dependent upon our choice to respect that person.

Those who work for me are not supposed to focus on *my* performance; they are supposed to concentrate on whether or not they do what they are paid to do.

Today, many employers beg good people to come to work. All a person needs to do is go to work, do a good job, and respect his superiors. If an employer thinks he has found someone he can trust, that person will soon be up for a promotion! Employers always look for someone to whom they can give something, and every employee that gets promoted is noticed because he learned to multiply his life investment with one common quality — *respect.*

When I address those who have been placed in authority over me

— even if they are much my junior in age — I say, "Yes, Sir" and "No, Sir" or "Yes, Ma'am" and "No, Ma'am." I also address people using "Mr." or "Mrs." all the time.

"Oh, no, he's just Bob."

Not to me, he isn't. He may be "Bob" to you, but he is "Sir" or "Mr. So-and-so" to me! To those who are over me in authority, I say, "Yes, Sir. Whatever you like, Sir. How would you like it done? What do you think about that?" I *don't* say, "Well, I think you're wrong about this." I have to recognize who I am in every relationship.

It's important to understand that the primary focus of your respect is not the person, but the position he or she holds. The person standing in front of me might act like he does not deserve one ounce of respect. But that does not matter to me; I show respect for him because I respect a *position* – what he represents to me. No matter what he does, he is in a place of authority. It is my responsibility to respect.

You must learn to honor and respect positions of leadership in the workplace without getting entangled in the "humanity" of personalities. As you esteem those who hold positions of authority, your reward is multiplied back to you.

DON'T CORRECT UPWARD

People do not realize how much they subtract from their position in the workplace when they refuse to respect those in authority over them. A person who lives in disrespect is at the height of his game already; he will never go any further in his vocation. His employer can't trust him because he always voices his own opinions and criticizes the way his employer does things.

That kind of disrespectful behavior inevitably causes the employer to become angry and edgy with the employee. The only antidote to this situation is this proverb: "A *soft answer turns away wrath...*" In other words, to change the relationship with his employer and get rid of the anger, that employee needs to become "soft" and respectful in the way he talks *to* his employer and about his employer to others.

Now, the employee might protest, "Yes, but my employer shouldn't be like that!" or "He's dealing with that situation all wrong!" I'm not saying an employer is always right in the way he carries out his responsibilities. What I am saying is that it is *not* the employees' job to tell him that he is wrong!

The moment we make our authority our rivals or our equals — the moment their opinions do not mean very much to us — is the moment they cease to be a doorway of wisdom, promotion, and increase in our lives. At that point, our employers can no longer teach us, because our disrespectful attitude has changed the posture of the relationship.

When we begin to ally with people who are in disagreement with our authorities in the workplace, we actually take steps backward and cause our authorities to take steps *away* from us.

Suddenly, our superiors start to look at us to see if our words match our actions. They are no longer sure they can trust us, for we have begun to allow mingled seed to be planted in our minds. We hear information from two directions — from our authorities and from those who criticize our authorities — and it causes us to become disloyal and disrespectful.

RECOGNIZING THE WISE IDENTIFIES THOSE FROM WHOM YOU CAN SAFELY ACCESS INFORMATION.

If we keep going in that direction, we will surely sabotage our promotion.

That's why it's so important that you adhere to this precept: **Recognizing the wise identifies those from whom you can safely access information.**

There are essentially two kinds of

people in your life — *yesterday people* and *tomorrow people*. *Yesterday people* are those who always want to drag you back into your past. They're not the people who inspire you to grow, nor do they cause you to change. They actually hinder you from becoming better. That's why it is easy to gravitate toward this kind of person when you are content with staying in mediocrity. They don't challenge you to grow — they are willing to accept you just the way you are.

But *tomorrow people* are those who are in your life to help you change. With these people, you may continually feel a certain pressure to change, to grow, to become better, and to move on to the next level. Don't feel like you aren't good enough for them. They are only trying to help you excel.

This is a healthy type of pressure, necessary in your life to help you become all you are intended to be. If you turn away from these people — those from whom you've been invited to access new information — and you become a companion of those who are disloyal and devoid of respect, you suffer the consequences. Solomon instructs us: *"He who walks with wise men will be wise, but the companion of fools will be destroyed."*

I have seen this principle operate in the workplace so many times. You just can't make strange bedfellows with discontented, disrespectful co-workers and succeed at the same time. Those people may harbor hidden motives that you will never understand. You really don't know why they became your friend. It's possible they did it just so they could undermine your position. **Make every effort to attach yourself to those who are respectful and moving forward — those who are really going somewhere with their life.**

In order to accelerate our growth in the workplace, we must (to a certain extent) give up what society calls our "rights." Otherwise, we won't be able to move up to the fullness of our greatest potential at our jobs. If we always try to protect our rights, we disdain anyone who intermittently makes us feel uncomfortable.

DON'T TAKE YOUR EMPLOYER FOR GRANTED

Taking your employer for granted ruins the harvest you are designed to receive from the field in which you have been placed.

Over-familiarity is often the culprit that causes us to take our authorities for granted and overstep our bounds with them. When that happens, our employers can no longer be a conduit of favor and growth in our lives. **Whatever or whomever becomes familiar to us becomes hidden to us.**

> NEVER ALLOW THE INVITATION TO INTIMACY TO BE DESTROYED BY THE CONTEMPT OF FAMILIARITY.

Whenever we go beyond our authority's invitation to intimacy, this reproach of familiarity attempts to invade our lives. It's a trap we do not talk much about, for it is very subtle. Gradually we become too familiar with the individuals who have been placed over us in life. As a result, we don't realize what we have in these people, until they are no longer a part of our lives.

Just because your employer invites you to a greater level of relationship with him doesn't mean you have been invited to have an opinion about the way he conducts himself in overseeing his responsibilities.

We also must learn not to listen to others who voice their negative opinions about these authority figures. We may never understand why our authorities do what they do or say what they say. But it isn't our responsibility to evaluate their decisions. I don't have a right to hold an opinion about those in authority, unless I have been asked to give it by those in authority. **Never harbor a negative opinion about people who are assigned to lead you.**

We are to stay out of the business of those who are above us. We have not been appointed to that level, so we shouldn't even go there.

Don't get your mouth and thoughts involved in matters with which you should not tamper.

"But I don't agree with what my employer is doing!" You may say. But what difference does it make whether or not you agree with your employer? Sure, I understand if something is being done unethically, but that is not what I am referring to. You weren't hired to fill that position of leadership, so you have no right to voice an opinion!

For many years, this has been a guideline I follow at the workplace: Whoever is the authority, I always agree with him. *I always side with my superiors.* Not to get something in return, but because I honestly believe they know more and have a better understanding of what must be done. Let's face it; if you were more qualified, wouldn't you be the boss?

I guarantee **if you take that position with your superiors in the workplace, you will stop trying to make decisions that are not your responsibility. This will prevent disrespect from destroying any future progress.**

DON'T MAKE STATEMENTS WITH YOUR QUESTIONS

One reason respect brings such good returns on your life investment is that it helps keep intact your relationships with your authorities. That is a goal many people fail to reach. They can start relationships, but very few know how to keep those relationships going.

Never allow yourself the luxury of questioning those who have chosen to employ you. Unless, of course, you have been invited to do so.

> NEVER ALLOW YOURSELF THE LUXURY OF QUESTIONING THOSE WHO HAVE CHOSEN TO EMPLOY YOU.

But never question your authority to your co-workers. What profit will it bring? None! Time is a great tattletale; time will tell whether or not your employer is right. You don't even need to think about it. Remember, his job is not to answer to you, so you never have to feel the need to check up on him.

When you trust in this manner and concentrate on staying respectful, you are able to avoid all arguments with your superiors. How is that possible? Because there is never a time when it is your place to challenge or complain about him. If you think you can give your employer his job description, why aren't you the employer? Since you aren't positioned to *be* the employer, you must *respect* him.

I assure you, complaining about your superior is *not* the way to multiply your assets at work and get promoted. Those who have the authority to advance you are not going to say, "Wow, thanks for telling me how bad your supervisor is! Since he isn't doing a good job, I'll make *you* the supervisor now!"

You do not want anything negative to come out of your mouth, because when you grumble, you do nothing but sow bad seed into your *own* life. Any complaints or criticisms that come out of your mouth will come back one day to smack you in the face and take away all you have gained thus far.

So, if you don't like the way your employer runs things at the job, do not question his ability to carry out his authority. Instead, ask yourself this important question: *Am I the employee I should be?* You will have plenty to keep you busy as you honestly seek the answer to *that* question!

WHEN YOUR EMPLOYER
IS A FAMILY MEMBER OR FRIEND

Throughout my experience in over two decades of human resource management, one thing I have seen again and again is the great number of employees who believe it is perfectly acceptable for them to be critical of employers because they are family or friends. They think, *"Since my employer and I are so close, that gives me the right to criticize the way he runs things."*

For some reason, these employees have the idea that they can say whatever they want to their employer. They also think they have the right to come in late. They even get upset and consider it an imposition if their employer asks them why they didn't arrive to work on time! It is absolutely unnerving to me to see how ungrateful such individuals can be.

No matter what your employer says or does, you don't have the right to be critical of him or her, no matter how familiar they are. You may ask, "Why would anyone act so disrespectfully toward their employers?" It's simple. They don't understand this important axiom: **You must never allow the comfort of familiarity to propagate the breach of disrespect.**

> NEVER ALLOW THE COMFORT OF FAMILIARITY TO PROPAGATE THE BREACH OF DISRESPECT.

When you work for an employer with whom you have another type of relationship, you need to be the very best employee your employer has ever had. You must not allow that familiarity to breed disrespect. You must work as a servant, not as a judge, with the motivation not of making money, but of making your employer and that business very prosperous. As you do this, you prosper as well.

Don't take advantage of an employer because he is a family member or your friend. Do just the opposite. You should take your personal time to serve him just because you want to!

This a whole new way of thinking, isn't it? You are the only one who can decide whether you are going to walk in respect or disrespect toward your employer. You are the only one who can make the choice to refuse to hold an opinion about your employer's decisions.

It's amazing to me how many employees tell me exactly what they think their employers do wrong. As they talk, I think, *"Wait a minute! If you are so far ahead of your boss, why isn't YOUR name on the sign in front of his office? Did you ever think for a moment that maybe there is a reason you aren't the person in charge? If you 'had the goods' to be the one in authority, then the powers that be would make sure you WERE in authority!"*

When a person is put in charge, he develops a whole new perspective on everything. Once he's in charge, he is not as opinionated as he used to be, because being the one in authority has a way of making a person more humble. Suddenly, that person figures out that there is more than one way to skin a cat. In other words, he recognizes that he may not necessarily make *right* decisions; he will try to make the *best* decisions he can.

> ALWAYS COVER YOUR LEADER'S SHORTCOMINGS. NEVER FLIPPANTLY EXPOSE THEIR MISTAKES.

The character of the student always comes out when the teacher makes a mistake. A respectful student realizes that he does not stop being a student, nor does he suddenly have the right to question his teacher's authority, just because his teacher made an error.

We live in a society that has such little respect for authority. That is why many people do not receive favor, promotion, or increase in their lives — because they do not understand the parameters of respect. They either don't realize or blatantly refuse to live by this principle:

Never exploit, bear tales, or have an opinion of your appointed leader, especially when he makes a mistake.

If your focus is on discovering and disclosing your employer's weaknesses and errors, your focus is on the person, not the *position*. Because of this improper focus, you begin to feel that you have the right to disrespect or question his wishes.

You know, long ago when I worked for a parcel delivery company, I made the decision that I would follow any of my supervisors' slightest wishes. Whenever my superiors opened their mouths with a request, I did my best to fulfill that request for them. One of my superiors made fun of me for that decision. He laughed at me and said, "Thompson, I'm going to bury you with work."

I said, "Excuse me, Sir, but you don't have enough work here to bury me. Whatever you'd like me to do, I'd be happy to do it for you. That's why I'm here, Sir. I'm here to get *you* a promotion. I'm here to make money for you. I'm not here to take anything from you. I'm here to *give* you something."

Some of my supervisors may not have liked me but none of them could control me. How could they control a man who would give them more than they even had the guts to demand? What bothered them more than anything else was that they could never upset me.

Other employees who worked with me used to get absolutely irate about the way some of the supervisors treated me. But I would say, "It's all right. We are to serve them all the more. We're here to serve. We're here to bless. We're here to *give* to them, not *take* from them." Choose the way of respect, and you will be blessed!

RESPECT YOUR FUTURE HARVEST

It is important that you live respectfully before others in the workplace, if you truly care about multiplying your life investment and protecting your future.

I have personally determined that I will not become weary in well doing. I will not throw in my hand and stop showing respect to those who are responsible over me. Therefore, I know that the ultimate harvest of my life will surely come!

Some people don't believe that. They have the idea that they will somehow be on the losing end if they show respect to people at their job. **You will find yourself in a better situation than you could have ever thought possible, if you will only live respectfully toward others!**

> RESPECT
> FOR YOUR PRESENT
> ASSIGNMENT IS PROOF
> THAT YOU EXPECT
> A FUTURE HARVEST.

For me, it is very simple. I do what I am asked to do. I don't ask why I need to do it. I don't give my opinions to my authorities, unless I am asked. I just say, "Whatever you say, you're right. Just tell me what you'd like me to do. I may need clarification about what you're asking of me, but I will never challenge you." By maintaining that respectful attitude, I respect my future harvest, so I can become all I need to become. **Respect for your present assignment is proof that you expect a future harvest.**

So ask yourself these questions:

- *What am I doing with my life investment in the arena of respect?*
- *What quality of seed am I sowing into my relationships at my job?*
- *Are people at work better or worse because of how I treat them?*

The moment you embrace this vital principle and begin to truly respect those with whom you work and those who are over you in authority, your attitude in the workplace begins to change. It changes the way your employer views you. It changes the way your fellow employees view you. And it multiplies your opportunities for promotion as you launch into the next level at your job!

Chapter Four Summary

- One of the qualities that bring the greatest return on any investment in the workplace is *respect*. For instance, if you do not understand or respect your finances, money leaves you. You may earn a lot of money, but you will never be able to accumulate it. On the other hand, if you both understand and respect the value of money, it comes toward you and overtakes your life.

- Respect is a very interesting word. Society has spent the last forty years dismantling the meaning of the word *respect*. As a result, many people don't even know what this word means. They do not respect themselves, let alone someone else!

- Respect is a quality that lives on the inside of a person. The truth is, all of life is lived from the internal rather than from the external. In fact, I'll go so far as to say this: *The way a person looks on the outside is the way he lives on the inside.*

- Because respect is an inward quality, no one can make another into a respectful person. A person is respectful because he *chooses* to be respectful.

- This issue of respect makes a huge difference in the workplace, because *respect guarantees access.* A person who is respectful cannot be stopped, because respect is a seed.

- Success pursues those who are respectful. Promotion overlooks anyone who disrespects those in authority. Disrespect subverts rather than multiplies any investment a person has made at his job.

- Grace on a person's lips brings royalty and favor to his friendships and surroundings. The person who excels at being pure of heart and consistently speaks respectful words of grace in the workplace will not remain in the background.

- Employers always look for someone to whom they can give something, and every employee that gets promoted is noticed because he has learned to multiply his life investment with one common quality — *respect*.

- People do not realize how much they subtract from their position in the workplace when they refuse to respect those in authority over them. A person who lives in disrespect is at the height of his game already; he will never go any further in his vocation.

- *Yesterday people* are those who always want to make you comfortable. They're not the people who spur you on, nor do they cause you to change. They do not urge you to become better.

- *Tomorrow people* are those who are in your life to help you change. They are usually the authorities placed over you in the various arenas of life, including your employer at work.

- *Remember, whatever or whomever becomes familiar to us becomes hidden to us.*

- *I always side with my superiors.* I guarantee this: If you take that position with your superiors in the workplace, you will stop trying to make decisions that are not your responsibility to make. You will prevent disrespect from destroying your progress.

- You are the only one who can decide whether you are going to walk in respect or disrespect toward your employer. You are the only one who can make the choice to refuse to hold an opinion about your employer's decisions.

- The moment you embrace this vital principle and begin to truly respect those with whom you work and those who are over you in authority, your experience in the workplace begins to change.

PRINCIPLES FOR RESPECT

* Respect Is Magnetic; It Attracts What You Crave, While Disrespect Pushes It Away.

* Disrespect Is The Thief That Steals Your Promotions.

* A Person Of Excellence Assesses Who And What He Is In Every Relationship And Then Postures Himself Accordingly.

* Never Correct Those Who Have Tolerated You In Your Present Position.

* Identify The Wise People From Whom You Should Access Information.

* Taking Your Employer For Granted Ruins The Harvest You Are Designed To Receive From The Field In Which You Have Been Placed.

* Never Allow The Invitation To Intimacy To Be Destroyed By The Contempt Of Familiarity.

* Never Hold An Opinion About People Who Are Assigned To Lead You.

* Never Allow Yourself The Luxury Of Questioning Those Who Have Chosen To Employ You.

* Never Allow The Comfort Of Familiarity To Propagate The Breach Of Disrespect.

* Always Cover Your Leader's Mistakes And Shortcomings. Never Expose Your Authority's Nakedness.

* Never Exploit, Bear Tales, Or Have An Opinion Of Your Appointed Leader, Especially When He Makes A Mmistake.

Promotion:
Making Your Dream A Reality

PROMOTION MUST BE EARNED—
IT IS NOT A
RESULT OF OUR EXISTENCE.

Promotion comes to those who earn it, not just because they want it. In America, it is easy to believe we should be rewarded for showing up. Many believe you should receive a bonus for being employed through December. There is no value to that type of bonus or raise. It is no different than going to the nearest trophy store and purchasing a first place trophy to show all your buddies. We must look for the reward that we earn through faithfulness and going the extra mile.

Any promotion that we receive unethically or through cutting corners eventually will be taken away from us. However, if we earn a promotion through hard work, there is no level we will not attain at our workplace. Author and speaker Isreal Salantar said, *"Promote yourself but do not demote another."*

BE EFFICIENT

Always look for ways to do higher quality and quantity of work within the same amount of time. You might have to work longer hours, but make sure those extra hours are used to go the extra mile. Let me give you an illustration to prove this point. Two farmers go out with the same intention – to produce a harvest that will generate revenue and food. Farmer A plants the seed, but never takes the time to cultivate the soil or look after the seed. He plants and does nothing to ensure there is a harvest. He intends to get a harvest, but isn't willing to pay the price to produce a great harvest. Farmer B cultivates the soil, plants the seed, and watches over the soil to ensure that seed he plants produces a harvest. He doesn't leave anything to chance.

What farmer deserves the harvest? Farmer B, of course. Farmer A didn't do anything to rightfully earn a harvest. What makes it any different when it comes to receiving a promotion? If you are like Farmer A, stop looking to reap what you did not sow. Just planting the seed is not enough to produce a harvest. You must look after it on a daily basis.

I love to dream. I love to take a look into the future at all that I believe I can become and all my life's purpose can accomplish. I realize that I cannot just dream. I need to make my dreams come to pass. It will not do me any good if I can't take my dream and transfer it into the natural realm, so I can walk it out day by day.

But *how am I going to make my dream of promotion come to pass?* It is easy to dream, but to walk it out is another story. Unless you remain focused and serious about attaining it, you will live in despair never truly realizing your complete potential.

It is amazing how many individuals have short commitment spans, never sticking with their dreams long enough to see them come to pass. They get all excited at the prospect of success, but are unable to walk it out.

Success principles only frustrate a person who is unwilling to apply them. Learning these principles of promotion will disappoint you if you do not act upon what you learn. You will know what to do, yet see no results.

> REWARDS ARE NEVER GRANTED FOR CONVERSATION BUT FOR COMPLETION.

The truth is if we only *hear* principles of success without *doing* them, we are what I like to call 'hope-peddling' ourselves. Therefore it remains true, that **rewards are never granted for the intention but the demonstration of what we say we can achieve.**

THE POWER OF YOUR INNER IMAGE

No longer do you need to live seeking the proverbial spotlight. Perhaps you have been dealt a deathblow. You may have been told that you aren't going to make it in your career or business, and that you are doomed to fail. You must turn a deaf ear to those lies, and focus only on today. If those lies have been bombarding your mind, stop believing them! Says Joel A. Barker, *"Those who say it can't be done are usually interrupted by others doing it."*

Your background doesn't matter. It does not matter what nationality or race you are. It does not matter that you were born underprivileged, or without societal refinements, pedi-

> YOU ARE DESTINED TO WIN; WHETHER OR NOT YOU DO IS UP TO YOU.

grees, or advantages. You were designed to live beyond all biases and prejudices. Go after your dream! Promotion will become a reality!

That's why it doesn't matter what anyone at the job says or thinks about you. It doesn't matter if people say you are at a disadvantage because you don't have the necessary background, education, training, or experience. You may have been surrounded by people who failed to realize their vocational dreams, but that doesn't mean you have to fail.

I made the decision long ago that it does not matter how I was raised. It doesn't matter who you think I am. I'm going to win! You may not be able to see the full manifestation of my victory right now, but stay by the sidelines and watch — because I am going to win! Remember this: It takes just as much effort to breathe and *lose* as it does to breathe and *win*, and I'm not destined to lose! Neither are you!

You have to develop this same confident trust in your ability to succeed. It doesn't matter what others think or say about it. All that matters is what you believe about yourself, and how determined you are to see your dreams come true. Eleanor Roosevelt observed, *"The future belongs to those who believe in the beauty of their dreams."* I like those words penned by Mrs. Roosevelt, but the missing component in her words is one's self-portrait. In fact I believe achievement is contained in the equation QSP = LA. **Your level of achievement (LA) in life is completely dependent upon the quality of your self portrait (QSP).**

How do you view yourself? Perhaps you focus on the way you look on the outside, thinking, *"You're so unworthy. You can't make it. You're too stupid. You just can't get on top of things, can you? It works for everyone else, but it has never worked for you."* Those kinds of thoughts are not going to help you realize your dream of promotion!

> YOUR LEVEL OF ACHIEVEMENT IN LIFE IS COMPLETELY DEPENDENT UPON THE QUALITY OF YOUR SELF PORTRAIT.

Over the years I have seen a common thread that runs through every successful individual: *They all have a positive self-image.* A positive self-image has nothing to do with race or creed. It isn't contingent on what kind of background a person has or on what side of the tracks he was born. A positive attitude about one's self originates in a person making the choice to *believe he is destined for greatness*.

So don't pick up your identity from your family or your background. Identify with the seed of greatness that is within you. Reject every thought that tells you that you are not going to achieve your dreams. **God intended for you to reach your full potential, but it will only happen when you *see yourself as a winner*!**

FAITHFULNESS:
DEDICATION, EVEN WHEN NO ONE IS WATCHING

One of the most important qualities you must possess in order to build a solid foundation of excellence in your life is *faithfulness*. There is a proverb that says: *"Most men will proclaim each his own goodness, but who can find a faithful man?"* That's a very good question — one that most employers constantly ask!

Many times people complain, "My supervisor doesn't like me, and I know that's the reason I'm not receiving a promotion." Truthfully the supervisors I talk to don't really care about someone's personality; they care about the quality of their work and their productivity.

Having the most charismatic person- ality in the whole company does not guarantee you a promotion. Your employer does not look to promote per- sonalities. Your employer looks to com- mit positions of responsibility to *faithful and productive employees*.

I know some people who are *very* talented. These people can hit a home run every time! The problem is

> IT IS IMPOSSIBLE FOR INTENTIONS TO PRODUCE A PROMOTION, BUT PRODUCTIVITY IS THE CONDUIT THROUGH WHICH YOUR FUTURE BECOMES ENRICHED.

it's hard to find them to put them up to the plate to bat!

A person like that says, "I'll be there at three o'clock." So you wait for him as the clock ticks away: four o'clock, five o'clock, six o'clock… Finally, he shows up and gives his excuse: "Oh, I'm sorry, I got caught up in something else. I tell you what — let's just do it tomorrow."

"All right, no problem," you say. "We'll go ahead and do it tomorrow."

The next day, it starts all over again. As you wait one, two, even three hours for this person to show up, you start thinking, *"You know, I really love this guy's work, but he never does what he says he will do!"*

Leaders cannot commit anything to undependable "hot shots." Employers delegate positions of responsibility to those who produce, not those who don't. Therefore it is very important that, **you must get results, never give regrets.**

> YOU MUST GET RESULTS,
> NEVER GIVE REGRETS.

A *faithful* man enjoys promotion, but the person who simply goes to work for the money ultimately is the loser. Now, I know that doesn't seem to make sense to your natural mind. You may wonder, *"But don't we all go to work so we can earn a paycheck?"*

So many people in today's world live for their time *off* instead of for their time *on* the job. They spend much more time thinking about their vacation than what they can produce at their place of employment.

But you cannot do that if you want to be known as a *faithful* person in the workplace. **Each time you enter the workplace, you must passionately pursue what your contribution will be never what your reward should be.**

> EACH TIME YOU ENTER
> THE WORKPLACE,
> YOU MUST PASSIONATELY
> PURSUE WHAT YOUR
> CONTRIBUTION WILL BE,
> NEVER WHAT YOUR
> REWARD SHOULD BE.

Strive to get yourself on the same side of the table as your boss and view your assignments from *his* perspective. Say to him, "Sir, how can I be more productive for you? I'll do the job no one else wants!" Your goal must be to make your boss the most successful person in his field and to get him a promotion. With an attitude like that, *your* promotion is guaranteed.

SEVEN SUREFIRE WAYS TO GET A PROMOTION

Moving up the corporate ladder isn't as hard as most people believe. As you know, promotion is a result, not a gift. It is a result of doing things right and doing them in excellence. Therefore I have outlined seven surefire ways to qualify for the promotion you want.

Surefire Ways To A **PROMOTION**

Personal Appearance

Attention to Detail

Personal Accountability

Complete Honesty

Career Expertise

Unbroken Focus

Exceed Expectations

1. Take Care Of Your Personal Appearance

The owner of one of the largest temporary employment agencies in America stated, "More than 98 percent of people are hired for their jobs because of personal appearance." This caused me to ask myself:

- *How do I look when I go to work in the morning?*
- *What can I do to take a step up to another level in my personal appearance?*

Your appearance is the first thing people notice about you, so why not use it to your advantage? Although many people dress how they feel, I made a commitment a long time ago to always dress how I want to feel. When you dress successful, you feel successful. An excellent appearance alters the flow of favor in your direction and attracts opportunities that otherwise would not be available to you. I find it interesting that people dress better for their interviews than they do after they get hired.

> YOU WILL NEVER BE REWARDED FOR YOUR SIMILARITIES TO ANOTHER, ONLY FOR YOUR DIFFERENCES FROM ANOTHER.

2. Become An Expert On Your Job

Educate yourself concerning your career path. Read magazine articles, newspaper clippings, and books that pertain to your job. Develop and hone the necessary skills to further advance you beyond your contemporaries. Focus your attention on becoming an expert in the field in which you work. **You will never be rewarded for your similarities to another, only for your differences from another.**

3. Give Special Attention To Detail

Promotion is summoned to your life the moment you give careful attention to detail. Suppose you walk down an aisle at work and see a piece of paper lying on the floor. Would you pick it up off the floor? Or would you leave it there and think, "That's job security for the maintenance man!" Although this may seem a small issue, it's not. This small detail is really important to those in authority at the workplace.

I don't take these small details lightly. I have had many business owners tell me, "You know, that's right. I do look for employees who don't neglect the little details." If you desire your employer to be impressed with you, then give immediate and accurate attention to the instructions he speaks to you. Immediate attention to detail gets you sure recognition.

As companies downsize, more and more people lose their jobs. How do you make sure that you're not one of them? Security comes by giving attention to detail. Every employer wants to surround himself with people who will not overlook the small details of their assignments, who follow an instruction and get it done quickly. Carefully look over every email, every project, every written proposal to ensure that you have carefully taken care of the little mistakes that can be made. It is important to see the value of focusing on the details. **Just one little mistake can wipe away years of achievement and trust.**

Let me just put it into perspective. Multiple 3 four times: 3 x 3 x 3 x 3 = 81. Now take 4 and multiple it four times: 4 x 4 x 4 x 4 = 256. That is a difference of 200%. That is the power of a small thing making a big difference. What about the surgeon who is nonchalant about the details of the open-heart surgery or the plane technician who overlooks the details? Small mistakes can have big consequences.

4. Remain Focused On The Assigned Task

Focus is the doorway to promotion. In a recent study, about 80 percent of employees and managers studied exhibited low focus and sporadic completion. Only twenty percent consistently followed through to completion. The difference was their ability to focus single mindedly on one task until they completed it. An author of Proverbs says, *"Let your eyes look straight ahead and your eyelids look right before you."* The reason so many fail to complete or accomplish their goals and dreams is broken focus. Speaker Dr. Mike Murdock says it like this, *"The only reason men fail is because of broken focus."*

Author James Allen said, *"You will become as small as your controlling desire, or as great as your dominant aspiration."* Where are you going? What is it you want to accomplish in the workplace? Having a goal or a finish line upon which to focus gives the necessary ingredients to experience the power of completion.

5. Never Require Oversight But Always Welcome Inspection

Employees that don't require oversight are rare. About 83 percent of today's employee population cannot work without direct oversight. They have to have someone looking over their shoulder eight hours a day. Another 14 percent need little oversight. So if you are a problem solver, you have nowhere to go but up in the company for which you work. Become the 3 percent that go over and above what is asked with no oversight necessary.

Employers no longer have time to micro-manage their employees. Your boss must know that you will get the job done and that he can trust you to do it in excellence. As a man or woman of integrity, you should have nothing to hide. Be willing to open yourself to personal examination. It creates a trust with your boss, and it keeps you from ever moving in the wrong direction.

Embrace examination! In fact, pursue it. Go to your boss openly and ask him to examine your work. Let him know that you would like to be a better employee, but you need him to let you know what to improve upon. As he corrects your work, accept the correction. Refuse the temptation to justify yourself. Make certain you don't become defensive. Listen carefully for a better way of doing what you have been asked to do.

6. Do More Than Is Expected Of You

Many refer to the concept of doing more than paid to do as "going the extra mile." Doing your best is great, but this idea of doing more than is expected of you goes one step further. Although you may do your best concerning what is required of you, it may not get you promoted.

You arrive at promotion when you do more than what is required. Just because the boss didn't ask you to do something does not mean you aren't supposed to do it. Take the initiative and go the extra mile. **Promotion is never granted by performing the tasks you are already paid to do. It comes by doing more than is expected of you.**

If you want to rise to new levels, you must move from conversation to demonstration. **You are only rewarded for that which you complete, not what you intend to get done.** You are always rewarded in direct proportion to your productivity. What are you accomplishing? Are you doing more than asked of you? Have you expected rewards for uncompleted assignments? Let your actions speak. There is no need to tell your boss what you can do. Simply under-promise and over-perform.

> AN EXCELLENT EMPLOYEE MAKES THE CHOICE TO GO FROM CONVERSATION TO DEMONSTRATION.

7. Be Honest About Mistakes

If you make a mistake, go to your superior and let him know what happened. Don't succumb to the pressure to blame-shift or put the responsibility for your mistakes on someone else. Remember this, admission stops prosecution. Tell on yourself. Tell your boss, "Sir, I made a mistake and I am willing to do whatever is necessary to correct it." When you display a humble attitude, you are trusted, respected, and favored.

Everyone makes mistakes, but only those who are willing to admit them continue on the journey of success. Don't hide your mistakes. Ultimately they will come to the surface, so be quick to admit and quick to seek correction. And when you are corrected, accept and follow the instruction to the 't'. If you do this, no employer will have a problem giving you a promotion.

I have just outlined seven simple practices you can immediately implement in order to qualify for promotion. Be patient, it does takes time to implement each area into your life, but the results will be amazing. Get ready; promotion is within your reach!

Be An Asset To Your Employer

Every day you go to work, you are there to be a problem solver in any way you can. That is what I endeavored to do years ago, while working at the parcel delivery service that I previously mentioned. When I first went to the company to apply for a job, I had just been released from the mental institution after having a life-changing spiritual awakening. I had no job, no money, no experience — I seemed to have nothing of value to offer the company. But I went over anyway, and filled out an application.

My heart sank, as I looked at all the questions on the application. The first one was, "Have you ever been on drugs?" (I checked the "Yes" box.) "Have you ever had a bad back?" (Another "Yes.") "When was the last time your back hurt you?" (I wrote "Recently.") "Have you ever had mental problems?" (Here we go again: "Yes.") "Have you ever been institutionalized?" ("Yes" again!)

The interviewer just watched me, as I checked all those "wrong" answers. But, amazingly, when I completed the application, he said, "Okay, you're hired!"

"But," he added. "You need to shave off your beard."

Now, when I heard that, I didn't start a class-action lawsuit. I didn't say, "Well, I'm going to get a bunch of people together to protest, because we want to keep our beards!" No, I just asked the man, "Do you have a razor? I'll do it right now." You see, from the very beginning, I was determined to be pleasing.

However, I had been hired as Christmas help. That meant when December 24th came, it was time to say good-bye! It was hard to go when the company laid me off on Christmas Eve. I loved my job there. I thought it was the greatest company in the world to work for, and enjoyed every moment of it.

When the company laid me off, my supervisor said, "Maybe you'll have the chance to work here again in a few months. We'll call you if we have an opening." But I didn't wait for them to call me; I called *them* — twice a week.

I said, "I just want to let you know one thing. I came here to work for your company because I'm good for you. I'm here to make you money. I want to help bring your company further along than you've ever been before. And I just want to let you know that you will never have one problem with me. I want to be a solution, not your problem."

Well, they hired me again, and I made good on my promise. I went to my supervisor every morning and said, "Boss, I want to tell you exactly why I'm here today. I am not here to earn money. I am here for the express purpose of getting you a promotion." I didn't care if I received a promotion. I wasn't trying to be a good employee just so I could get ahead. I worked for my supervisor's promotion.

When you labor for another's promotion, someone is mysteriously assigned to accelerate yours.

Continue to pursue excellence in all that you do. No man can keep you from being promoted just because you don't live by his lower standards. Allow *excellence* and *integrity* to bring you up to the level you desire at your

> WHEN YOU LABOR FOR ANOTHER'S PROMOTION, SOMEONE IS MYSTERIOUSLY ASSIGNED TO ACCELERATE YOURS.

job. When you do it the principled way — when you refuse to be controlled or manipulated, but faithfully serve instead — you *will* be promoted. You will not only go to a higher level at work; you will remain at that higher level once you reach it. *That's* how you fulfill your dream of promotion and success in the workplace!

Chapter Five Summary

- Success principles only frustrate a person who does not apply them to his life. Learning these principles condemns you if you do not act upon them, because you know what to do, yet will not do it. The truth is if we only hear principles of success without doing them, we are living in a pipe dream.

- Joel A. Barker, *"Those who say it can't be done are usually interrupted by others doing it."*

- Your background doesn't matter. It does not matter what nationality or race you are. It does not matter that you were born underprivileged, or without societal refinements, pedigrees, or advantages. You were designed to live beyond all biases and prejudices. Go after your dream! Promotion CAN become a reality!

- I made the decision long ago that it does not matter how I was raised. It doesn't matter who you think I am. I'm going to win!

- Don't allow one thought to stay in your mind that tells you you are not going to achieve your dreams. You have been created to reach your full potential, but it will only happen when you see yourself as a winner!

- A faithful man enjoys promotion, but the person who simply goes to work for the money ultimately is the loser.

- Every day you go to work, you are there to be a problem solver in any way you can.

- Continue to pursue excellence in all that you do. No man can keep you from being promoted just because you don't live by his lower standards. Allow excellence and integrity to bring you up to the level you desire at your job.

PRINCIPLES FOR PROMOTION

- Rewards Are Never Granted For The Intention But Rather For The Demonstration Of What We Say We Can Achieve.

- We Are Destined To Win; Whether Or Not We Do Is Up To Us.

- Your Level Of Achievement In Life Is Completely Dependent Upon The Quality Of Your Self Portrait.

- It Is Impossible For Intentions To Produce A Promotion, But Productivity Is The Conduit Through Which Your Future Becomes Enriched.

- You Must Get Results, Never Give Regrets.

- Each Time You Enter The Workplace, You Must Passionately Pursue What Your *Contribution* Will Be, Never What Your *Reward* Should Be.

- When You Labor For Another's Promotion, Someone Is Mysteriously Assigned To Accelerate Yours.

Productivity:
Adding Value
In The Workplace

NEVER LOOK FOR ANOTHER ASSIGNMENT
UNTIL YOU SUCCESSFULLY
COMPLETE YOUR LAST AND
MOST IMPORTANT ONE.

If you've gotten this far, it is safe to say you have set some important goals for yourself at your place of employment, and you probably have a good idea of what you want to achieve. More than likely you have a desire to be promoted to a higher position with greater responsibility. Here are a few questions to ponder:

- *How are you going to make your dream of promotion come to pass?*
- *What steps are you going to take to ensure future promotion?*
- *Do you have a plan?*
- *What are you currently doing that makes you believe you are deserving of one?*

These are questions that must be answered. Personally, I love to dream. I love to think about the possibilities ahead and about all I want to accomplish in my lifetime. Still, I realize that achievement is only produced when I leave the dream realm and take action. This chapter is written to help you become more productive so you can fulfill your dreams.

TRUTHS DISCOVERED

It amazes me how many individuals quit striving toward their goals. After all, the bigger the dream, the greater the distance you must travel. **The most miserable people in the world today are those who know what they need to do to create the life they desire, but they refuse to take the actions to do so.**

Throughout my life, I have discovered three simple, career-enhancing truths:

First, assess the desired outcome of the project.

Second, assess what action must be taken immediately.

Third, concentrate entirely on the most important task until it is complete.

In today's business culture, productivity is the key to promotion. Without productivity all the other pursuits in this book won't mean a thing because every employer (by reason of economics) is forced to look at the bottom line.

Let's take a look at these three keys to guaranteed productivity.

1. Assess the desired outcome of the project.
What is considered a successful outcome of a particular project or task? The clearer the desired result, the quicker you can take action. Always be certain you are on the same page as your employer regarding the desired outcome of a task. Don't assume the outcome you desire is the

outcome your boss does. There is no substitute for double-checking and communication so you and those who write the checks are moving in the same direction.

2. Assess what actions must be taken immediately.

You may have ten, fifteen, or even fifty things on your plate to do right now, but do you know what to do next? Identifying the next action takes a matter of minutes, but is often a highly neglected practice. Look over your list of projects and ask yourself, what must I do next? Write it down. After you go through your projects and write out each action step, determine the highest priority and get to work.

You cannot do *everything* right now. All that matters is what you do right now and what you must do next. A great question to ask is, *"What action if done will be of the most benefit to you and the company?"* or, *"What action if not done will be most detrimental to your career success?"*

3. Concentrate entirely on the most important task until it is complete.

Quickly solve every problem that comes your way and soon your stock will rise in the eyes of those who are looking for someone to promote. Allow time and your track record to speak on your behalf. Don't force the issue. Your ability to act quickly and get more done than anyone else will cause you to stand out.

If you can create a memory in your supervisor's mind that you are a person who can get the job done quickly and in excellence, more responsibility and opportunity will be given to you. Getting the job done quickly may mean the difference between you or someone else getting a promotion.

One way of ensuring that you focus on the right things is by simply asking questions! Here are some questions you could ask:
- *What is the purpose of my job?*
- *What are the measures of success at my job?*
- *What is an exceptional performance to me?*

- *What are the priorities of my supervisor?*
- *What resources are available to me?*
- *What costs are acceptable?*

Remember, your boss's time is valuable, so be straight and to the point. Ask these questions, write down his answers, and thank him for his time. If the conversation is going to carry on, allow him to drive it.

Results matter. According to Anthony Robbins, you always succeed when producing a result. Getting the job done matters. You get paid for results, not for sincere intentions. A high percentage of those who rise to the top of organizations make their mark by being productive and doing their job with excellence. The more productive you are the quicker you will be promoted.

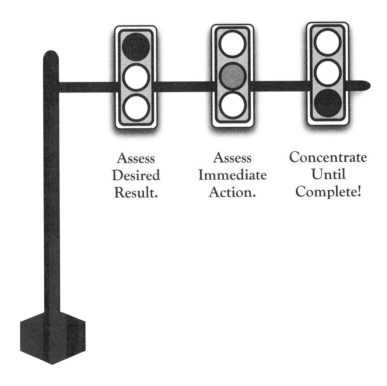

Assess	Assess	Concentrate
Desired	Immediate	Until
Result.	Action.	Complete!

PRODUCTIVITY REQUIRES TIME MASTERY

The most common form of stress people experience is anxiety from too much to do and too little time to do it. In fact, time issues are the greatest struggle in the workplace. There is simply not enough time to do everything that needs to be accomplished. Because of budget limits, lack of human resources, and competitive pressures, employees are required to perform at higher levels while taking on more and more work, all of which is urgent, necessary, and important.

The solution to this problem is the ability to master your time. You aren't going to get more than 24 hours; tasks won't decrease, and time won't stop. Therefore, learning to manage your time is the only option.

Regardless if you feel you know how to manage your time effectively, there is always room to grow. Here are a few principles that you can immediately apply to become one of the most productive and efficient employees at your job.

1. **The investment of time is the first prerequisite to performing your duties in excellence.**
Don't waste time by doing something half-hearted. Give it everything you have. Make the final product a memory of your best rather than a reminder of corners cut. Time once used is gone forever. The only way to live without regret is to do your best with what you have. Give your best effort and you will never be disappointed.

Martin Luther said, "*If a man is called to be a street sweeper, he should sweep streets even as Michelangelo painted or Beethoven composed music or Shakespeare wrote poetry. He should sweep streets so well that all the host of heaven and earth will pause to say, 'here lived a great street sweeper who did his job well.'*"

2. Value time as you value money.

What you respect comes toward you and what you disrespect moves away from you. If you do not respect your time, you will not enjoy your future. No great future is promised to those who disrespect their time in the present. Cherish time and you will be richly rewarded.

Do you know where your time goes? Can you account for how you used your time this past week? The more you value it, the more benefit it brings to your life. Remember, the poor and rich both have twenty-four hours; the only difference between the two is the value they place upon each second.

3. Document your time on a weekly basis.

Do you know where your time goes? Make up a time log, and keep an accurate daily record for one month. You'll be amazed at the amount of time you use unwisely.

This is the same application finance consultants use to teach people to manage their money. When people don't know where their money goes, they believe that they don't have enough of it. When people don't know where their time goes, they think the same thing.

Logging your time may prove you manage your time well, but what if you have 30, 40, or even 60 hours of unaccounted time each week? That could mean the difference between an annual salary of $30,000 or $50,000. Where your time goes does matter. I have counseled hundreds of individuals who have told me they didn't have enough time to do everything that needed to get done. They wanted to lessen their commitments, thinking that would solve their problems.

> THE LACK OF TIME CAN'T PRODUCE FAILURE. ONLY MISMANAGED TIME CAN.

We have a tendency to take as long as we have to get something done. For example, go back to your school days. Did you ever have a paper assigned to you at the beginning of the month, but then waited until the night before it was due to write it? I have. That's what many employees do in the workplace. **The mother of failure is never the lack of time but most often the mismanagement of it.**

This month, create a detailed log of your time. At the end of the month, make a pie chart of all the things you put time into. You'll see how much time you really have. The same individuals who tell me they don't have time realize they have more time than they know what to do with. To their surprise they usually have between 15 to 30 hours of unaccounted time per week.

Most people spend 80% of their time on issues that don't really matter and only 20% of their time on truly significant tasks. How does that happen? Because people mistake urgent for important. Discerning the difference between what is urgent and what is important is the most difficult challenge to time mastery.

4. Budget your time.
Once you understand where your time goes, you must learn how to budget it to get the most out of it. You have 168 hours per week. How you spend those hours is your choice. Budgeting your time begins with a plan. Plan your day and then diligently work your plan. Take time every morning to plan out your day. Five minutes spent planning may save you hours by the end of the day.

Prioritize each task and schedule a time when you will complete it. There is no "one plan fits all," but any plan is better than no plan. Research suggests that one minute of planning is equivalent to ten minutes of production. Budget your time every morning before you start your workday. Write down everything you need to get done, and assign a time slot for each task.

5. Make it known — "My time must be respected."
This is the key to fighting off those time vampires, the individuals who

waste your time with endless conversation and pointless interruptions. Everyone should not have the same access into your life. Others should have to earn or qualify for your time. You cannot simply visit the President of the United States because you want to. You must qualify for his time. Why should it be any different for your time? It shouldn't. Don't allow co-workers to waste your time. Make it known that your time must be respected.

People will waste your time unless you protect it. You don't have to send out a mass memo; simply let others know you need to get things done. Set beginnings and endings to your meetings to let others know that you run a tight schedule. Then you have the power to extend your meeting depending upon if it is productive. Otherwise, they can either write you an email or schedule another meeting.

If you do not convey to others that your time is valuable, they will almost always waste it. The moment they know you don't waste time they will begin to respect it. They will honor you for it. They won't be offended by it. When they spend time with you, they will be clear and precise because subconsciously they know your time is valuable.

6. Invest your time with experts of your chosen field.

You must do whatever is necessary to get time with those wiser than you. Find a way to pursue the knowledge and expertise of those who hold the position you want. Send them a gift with a letter asking them for a time during which you can ask questions to glean from their wisdom. They have what you need, not the other way around, and they are keys to your future. Posture yourself as a student ready to listen. They will teach you what to do and what not to do. Learn from their mistakes and determine not to make the same.

7. Take time out of your day to grow as a person.

You need time to be alone. It is not selfish to look after yourself. You cannot help anyone when you are not taken care of. The time you take to develop your character and hone your skills will open doors of opportunity for you.

Is has been said that the difference between achievers and non-achievers is what they do during the time slot of 6:00 to 9:00 p.m. While non-achievers watch television, achievers may learn a new skill. **Your promotion begins at the workplace, but it certainly doesn't end there.** It carries on through the rest of your day.

8. Take time to plan your day.

Planning your day ahead of time increases your productivity by nearly 25%. Remember, *those who fail to plan, plan to fail.* Become part of the small percentage that refuses to live out their day before it is on paper. Author and speaker, Dr. Mike Murdock says, *"The secret of your future is hidden in your daily routine."*

9. Have a vision for life.

I believe that the first step in time management is a vision for your life. Let me explain it like this: Time is like a closet. Every hour is a shelf that needs to be filled. When arranging your closet, you must keep in mind how you want things to look. How do you want your closet to look in the end? The picture you have influences where you put your things. The same holds true with your time. A picture of where you want to be in the coming future influences where your time goes.

If you don't have a clear picture of where you want to be, you won't be clear about where your time should go. The end result is a cluttered and disorganized life, never fully achieving your goals and realizing your dreams.

> TIME IS THE TAXI THAT DELIVERS YOU TO YOUR DESIRED DESTINATION.

Time mastery can only be accomplished after first establishing a purpose and vision for your life. If you do not know where you are going in life or why you are working, then what you do with your time does not matter to you. The moment you get a vision, you bring purpose into every minute, every hour, every day, and every week of your life.

Without the jigsaw puzzle box, you have a very difficult time determining where each piece goes. The picture on the box gives you an idea of which puzzle piece fits where. The same is true for your life and pieces of the puzzle called time. A foggy picture of where you are heading produces anxiety, caution, and insecurity. But those who have a clear picture of their future can confidently invest their time in the areas that move them in their desired direction.

10. Establish time constraints for everything you do.

Have a deadline for everything you do. For larger tasks, set up small goals to measure your progress. Putting time limits on your life may seem like an inconvenience at first, but you'll see the results in your work.

11. Stop being a time thief.

How does a person steal time from his employer? By showing up late. By talking with others while they are expected to work. By taking longer breaks than allotted. By handling personal matters on company time. By packing up fifteen minutes before work ends.

How can you steal your own time? By not planning it. Your time is your life, and it shouldn't be wasted. You may have already discovered that people don't care if they waste your time, so you have to be very protective of it. And if you protect your boss's time, others respect yours.

IVY LEE AND CHARLES SCHWAB

You have probably heard of the story of Ivy Lee and Bethlehem Steel, but I would like to share it to illustrate this point. Charles Schwab was the president of the company, a real high-achiever.

He actually was the first man to ever earn a million dollar yearly salary. Ivy Lee was a management consultant who wanted a contract with the company. Schwab rebuffed him, saying that they already knew more about producing and selling steel than Lee would ever know. Then he gave Lee a challenge that would go down in business folklore. Schwab told Lee that the only thing he himself lacked was the time to implement all the ideas he had and that if Lee would show him a way to get more things done with his time, he would pay him any fee within reason.

According to management expert Donald Schoeller, Lee replied, "Write down the most important tasks you have to do tomorrow and number them in order of importance. When you arrive in the morning begin at once on number 1 and stay on it until it is completed. Recheck your priorities; then begin with number 2. If any task takes all day, never mind. Stick with it as long as it is the most important one. If you don't finish them all, you probably couldn't do so with any other method and without some system, you'll probably not even decide which one was most important. Make this a habit every working day. When it works for you, give it to your men. Try it as long as you like. Then send me your check for what you think it is worth."

What he said is so unbelievably simple that you may find it hard to grasp its importance. Charles Schwab loved it. He sent Ivey Lee a check for $25,000, calling the advice the most profitable lesson he'd ever learned. He credited this system with turning around Bethlehem Steel and making it, in its day, the biggest independent steel producer in the world.

Business experts later chided Schwab for his extravagance in sending Lee so much more than he expected, but Schwab insisted that is the best investment he'd made all year, saying that it was only once he'd adopted this system that he found all of his people doing the most important things first.[1]

BENEFITS OF EFFECTIVE TIME MASTERY

People are motivated by two factors: benefits and consequences. I will briefly share with you five benefits of effective time mastery then share what I believe are the top three penalties of mismanaged time.

- **PROVIDES BALANCE.**

Balance is the reward provided to those who manage their time well. Many people live on one side or the other of the spectrum. Managing your time effectively allows you to balance every area of your life to the maximum.

- **BRINGS PROMOTION.**

There is a myth that those who work really long hours always get the promotion. That is not necessarily true because productivity is not directly proportional to the amount of time one works. Working long hours may just mean someone takes longer to get something done. Just because you clock out two hours after five doesn't mean that you are working harder. Only when you do more than you are paid to do in those extra couple of hours can you expect a promotion. Promotion belongs to those who manage their time well, while at the same time are overly productive.

- **RELIEVES STRESS AND ADDED PRESSURE.**

If you feel stressed or overwhelmed, the problem may not be that you have too much on your plate. You may just be unclear about the direction of a specific project; therefore you will not be confident in how you use your time.

Clarity accounts for fully 80% of success and happiness. More than any other, lack of clarity is probably the leading factor for underachievement and stress. Once you have an organized plan and purpose by which you manage your time, you will accomplish more and feel less stressed. The better you organize your workload and projects, the less stress and pressure you add to your life.

- ## MAKES ONE MORE RELIABLE.

Managing your time well enables you to do what you said you would do. How many times have you met someone who says, "I'll call you in a minute," and it takes him a couple of hours? Or have you met the person who says, "I'll meet you at 5:00 p.m.," and they show up at 5:20 p.m.?

Your ability to manage your time causes others to take you at your word. When you say you are going to be somewhere at a certain time, you must make sure you are there. If you tell someone you will call back shortly, make sure to call back as soon as you can. People trust you by how well you manage your time, so stay true to the time commitments you make.

- ## FAVOR COMES TO YOUR LIFE.

Favor is granted the moment the right person discovers that your performance exceeds your coworkers. Favor is not when someone dumps blessings into your life. Favor in a nutshell, gives you an opportunity to change your future. **Favor is the unknown desire that someone has to help you succeed.** It is when someone has a desire to participate in the outcome of your life. We need those who can take us to where we haven't been. Favor can only come from those who can promote us. Therefore we must seek to please those whom God has called us to serve.

Many think favor is "luck" or "good fortune" or perhaps even "chance." They do not understand that we are the determining factor for favor to enter our lives. An employer doesn't sit in his chair and say to himself, "Let's show favor to Jimmy today, but as for Barbara, we are not going to show her favor." There are principles to attain promotion. Doing these principles increases favor while neglecting them decreases favor.

PENALTIES OF POOR TIME MANAGEMENT

You must realize that you may suffer some possibly life changing consequences if you fail to master your time. Let's take a quick look at some of the consequences people suffer for not taking control of their time.

- ### LOSS OF OPPORTUNITY.

Without knowing it, you may spend the majority of your time on the least important things. If this is true in your life, you may squander plenty of opportunities.

Your promotion is waiting for you, but only when you begin to focus on the most important 20% will you ever be able to use it to your advantage. There are key assignments that when done quickly and in excellence cause your boss or supervisor to recognize you and grant you the promotion for which you have waited.

- ### LOSS OF ENERGY AND MOMENTUM.

We live in a hurried age. Our days are many times just a blur. We celebrate speed rather than quality. We race through our lives without pausing to consider who we want to be or where we want to go. We get things done, but we lose energy and momentum in the long run. Most of us try to do our best to manage our time and be productive, but we don't have the energy to sustain the high levels of productivity.

Jim Loehr, author of *The Power of Full Engagement*, says, *"When demand exceeds our capacity, we begin to make expedient choices that get us through our days and nights but take a toll over time. We survive on too little sleep, wolf down fast foods on the run, fuel up with coffee and cool down with alcohol and sleeping pills. Faced with relentless demands at work, we become short-tempered and easily distracted. We return home from long days at work feeling exhausted and often experience our families not as a source of joy and renewal, but as one more demand in an already overburdened life."*

An unbalanced life ultimately leads to an energy deficient life. When you feel tight on time, you neglect the things that are needed to sustain your life such as eating, sleeping, and laughing.

• LOSS OF SENSE OF WORTH.

Because your life is made up of time, the more you waste time or are unable to account for it, the more your self-worth diminishes. You cannot feel good if you waste your time. As you miss opportunities and lose valuable energy throughout your day, your self-worth decreases.

Managing Your Time Is Beneficial

Manage your time well and your life will go well. Manage your time poorly and your life will come to ruin. If you want to excel in your life and at your place of work, learn the keys to effective time mastery. Once you master this area, promotion in every area of life will soon become a reality.

> Promotion Is A Result Of Productivity, Not The Reward For Good Company.

Let me quickly reiterate that the reward of productivity is promotion. We live in a bottom line world and in order to achieve the promotion we desire, we are required to come through and produce results. **Promotion is a result of productivity, not the reward for good company.**

No one is born productive, but there are certain techniques you can learn to be more efficient in the workplace. There are many great methods to enhance productivity. Some of the techniques most commonly practiced by today's leading experts include:

- PRIORITIZE

Your ability to set clear and accurate priorities determines your level of productivity in the workplace. How do you know what is a high priority and what is not? By asking these two simple questions.

First, what one task if I do right now will add the most value to my company?

Second, what one task if not done will cause me to suffer the greatest consequence?

These answers will help you differentiate between what is important and what is urgent. You always want to make sure you put at least eighty percent of your focus on the top twenty percent of your tasks.

To be productive you must focus on the activities that add the most value to your work. These priorities must be clear and they must be written. Work from a list. Write down your tasks and activities on some type of paper or time management system. Some may argue, "I work best from my mind." That is not true. No one works best from their mind. You cannot properly organize or strategize in your mind. Take a moment and think of everything you have to get done. Every time you think of a new task the previous one is forgotten or has a chance to be forgotten. I have heard it said like this: a small pencil is better than a long memory. What I write down, I don't have to remember. This frees me from feeling like I have too many things on my plate.

The technique I prefer over others is to prioritize my work using the ABC method. I have learned through experience that when I don't prioritize my projects I don't accomplish what I set out to do. The ABC method is simple. All it requires is that you review your list of tasks before you begin and put an A, B, or C next to each task. Multiple tasks with the same letter are denoted by A1, A2, and so on. An "A" task is something that is very important. A "B" task is something you should do, but the consequences aren't as great as an "A" task. A "C" task is simply something you would enjoy doing, but these tasks do not have any immediate consequences. The rule of the technique is basic. Never do a "B" before an "A" and never do a "C" before a "B."

Ask your boss to help you prioritize; don't do it alone. Let your supervisor know, "This is what I have on my schedule, and you'd like me to fit in this new assignment. I need this much time to complete the new assignment. So where would you like me to put it in my schedule of tasks I need to complete for you?"

Setting priorities is not a burden; it helps you to know where you are and what still needs to be accomplished. You must work at it until it becomes natural.

Much of the stress in your work life comes from low-priority tasks.

The amazing discovery is that as soon as you start working on your highest-value activity, all your stress disappears. You feel a continuous stream of energy and enthusiasm. As you work toward the completion of something that is really important, you feel an increased sense of personal value and inner satisfaction.

- ### CONCENTRATE ON ONE THING AT A TIME

If you cannot focus single-mindedly on one task, you cheapen the quality of the final project. For many people it is difficult to focus on one thing before moving to the next. Productivity does not mean multi-tasking. It means completing task after task after task.

- ### ORGANIZE YOUR WORK ENVIRONMENT

Work from a clean desk. It causes your mind to be free from chaos. Up to thirty percent of office time is spent looking for misplaced items and papers. Time management experts encourage people to go through all their papers and decide what needs to be filed and what needs to be thrown away. Brian Tracey says, *"When in doubt, throw it out!"*

Your goal is to structure your area so you can work more efficiently. Supplies, tools, and information you use most often should be at your fingertips, readily retrievable and replaceable.

When you don't have the time to organize, the next best thing is to remove the clutter to a different place while you work. You feel more relaxed and focused. You will be amazed at the unnecessary things on your desk. We tend to put things on our desk that we don't really need. Instead of putting things where they belong, we throw them on our desk. Go through the things on your desk. What you don't need, throw away. Why keep unnecessary paperwork? This couple of hours used to organize will save you more than that per week.

- ### APPLY THE PARETO PRINCIPLE

In 1906, Italian economist Vilfredo Pareto created a mathematical formula to describe the unequal distribution of wealth in his country. He observed that twenty percent of the people owned eighty percent of the wealth. In the late 1940s, Dr. Joseph M. Juran accurately attributed the 80/20 rule to Pareto, calling it Pareto's principle. While it may be misnamed, Pareto's principle can be a very effective tool to help you manage effectively.

This law says that 20% of the things you do account for fully 80% of the value of all the things you do. In other words the 80/20 rule means that in anything, a few (20 percent) are vital and many (80 percent) are trivial. The reverse is that 80% of the things you do account for 20% of the value of all you do. You can't do everything, so focus on the twenty percent of tasks until completion.

Pareto's principle, the 80/20 rule, should serve as a daily reminder to focus eighty percent of your time and energy on the twenty percent of your work that is really important. Don't just work smart, work smart on the right things.

- **GET IT DONE NOW!**

There is never enough time to do everything, but there is always enough time to accomplish the most important things. No one works best while they're under pressure. People only believe that because it's all they know. Pressure leads to more mistakes and less time to fix them.

"Get it done now," is my personal motto. **If I can't do it now, I don't give any thought to it until I can.**

- **SPEED AND EXCELLENCE**

Refuse to delay or procrastinate on what is important. Your boss and those around you will notice your sense of urgency. You will soon develop a reputation for speed and dependability. When people need things done fast, they will come looking for you. Whenever you work on a task, always be proud to sign your name to it.

• BALANCE

There is more to life than work. Steven Covey, best selling author of *Seven Habits of Highly Effective People*, is known for saying, *"No one on their death bed is going to regret not working more."* Set aside time to do other things. Choose to leave your work at the office and focus on what really is important in your life. Work is important, but families are irreplaceable.

> THE KEY TO LIFE RESTS IN THE DELICATE ARMS OF BALANCE.

What are some things you can stop doing to free up time to do the important things of life? Make a decision and do it. Free up your time in order to do what will create the future you desire.

ENJOY LIFE

Life is enjoyed only when it is lived in balance. God placed you here on earth to enjoy His creation, not to live a stressed out and burdened life. What you learned in this section on productivity is not to motivate you to work more, but to work smarter and be more productive. You can get more done in less time and feel good about using other time to spend with family and friends.

Every area of life has to have the correct ingredients to truly be enjoyed. Your family must be in balance, your career must be in balance, your education must be in balance, and your spiritual life must be in balance. Life is like the spinning of a top. As long as the top spins straight, it is free from accident. When the top is out of balance, there is a quick spin out.

You must take an account of what transpires in your life to be certain you are balanced. This doesn't mean everything gets the same amount of time. Everything must get the right amount of time. Life does not allow for imbalance. You must make a commitment to maintain all areas of life. Proverbs tells us, "God abhors an imbalanced life."

Remind yourself continually what is really important. The reason you work is so that you can enjoy relationships and life itself. Work gives you the resources to do what you enjoy. Don't lose sight of the purpose of work. Relationships are everything. Fully eighty-five percent of all personal success is directly linked to those with whom you associate.

The keys to productivity are simple — **assess what is considered a successful outcome, take action immediately, and focus until completion.** The keys to success in life are also simple. Value God, yourself, people, and then work. Set those important to you as the most important use of your time. Make time for your family and friends. Put people before work, especially those who are important to you. Be productive all the time you are working, and when work is over, give yourself to the people you love.

Put just one of these principles into practice and you will become one of the most productive employees in your organization. Your promotion rests in your ability to master your time. Dr. Michael Leboeuf has this to say about time, *"Waste your money and you're only out of money, but waste your time and you've lost a part of your life."*

Chapter Six Summary

- Throughout my life, I have discovered three simple, career-enhancing truths: First, assess the desired outcome of the project. Second, assess what action must be taken immediately. Third, concentrate entirely on the most important task until it is complete.

- You may have ten, fifteen, or even fifty things on your plate to do right now, but do you know what to do next? Identifying the next action takes a matter of minutes, but is often a highly neglected practice. Look over your list of projects and ask yourself, what must I do next?

- If you can create a memory in your supervisor's mind that you are a person who can get the job done quickly and in excellence, more responsibility and opportunity will be given to you.

- The more productive you are, the quicker you will be promoted.

- The only way to live without regret is to do your best with what you have. Give your best effort and you will never be disappointed.

- The poor and rich both have twenty-four hours; the only difference between the two is the value they place upon each second.

- Most people spend eighty percent of their time on issues that don't really matter and only twenty percent of their time on truly significant tasks. How does that happen? Because people mistake urgent for important.

- People will waste your time unless you protect it. You don't have to send out a mass memo; simply let others know you need to get things done.

- Is has been said that the difference between achievers and non-achievers is what they do during the time slot of 6:00 to 9:00 p.m. While non-achievers watch television, achievers may learn a new skill.

- Dr. Mike Murdock says, *"The secret of your future is hidden in your daily routine."*

- Time mastery can only be accomplished after first establishing a purpose and vision for your life. If you do not know where you are going in life or why you are working, then what you do with your time does not matter to you.

- Manage your time well and your life will go well. Manage your time poorly and your life will come to ruin. If you want to excel in your life and at your place of work, learn the keys to effective time mastery.

- Your ability to set clear and accurate priorities determines your level of productivity in the work place.

- Pareto's principle, the 80/20 rule, should serve as a daily reminder to focus eighty percent of your time and energy on the twenty percent of your work that is really important. Don't just work smart, work smart on the right things.

- Life is enjoyed only when it is lived in balance. God placed you here on earth to enjoy His creation, not to live a stressed out and burdened life. What you learned in this section on productivity is not to motivate you to work more, but to work smarter and be more productive.

- Dr. Michael Leboeuf has this to say about time, *"Waste your money and you're only out of money, but waste your time and you've lost a part of your life."*

PRINCIPLES FOR PRODUCTIVITY

* → Assess What Action Must Be Taken Immediately.

* → Concentrate Entirely On The Most Important Task Until It Is Complete.

* → Invest Whatever Time Is Necessary To Produce The Highest Possible Level Of Excellence In Your Work.

* → Lack Of Time Can't Produce Failure. Only Mismanaged Time Can.

* → Failure Is The Not The Lack Of Time, But The Proof Of Mismanaged Time.

* → Time Is The Taxi That Takes You To Your Desired Destination.

* → Favor Is Granted To Anyone Who Rises Above The Performance And Productivity Of Their Counterparts.

* → Promotion Is A Result Of Your Productivity, Not A Reward For Your Good Company.

* → The Key To Life Rests In The Delicate Arms Of Balance.

Problem Solving:
Walking Toward The Rewards

PROBLEM SOLVING
IS DOING MORE THAN
YOU NEED TO, NOT BECAUSE YOU
HAVE TO, BUT BECAUSE YOU WANT TO.

No matter what kinds of circumstances we face, we were created to win. We have been equipped with the tools necessary to turn any losing situation into an ultimate triumph. Yet in spite of it all, many lose in the game of life. I have always been very interested in knowing why this is the case.

How do doors of opportunity and promotion open for us in life, so we can use our gifts and abilities to their fullest extent?

EVERYTHING CREATED SOLVES A PROBLEM

Do you realize that every single thing on earth was created to solve a problem? Living organisms solve food chain problems, new inventions solve man-made problems, and so forth.

In the workplace, different occupations solve different problems.

- Doctors solve health problems.
- Dentists solve dental problems.
- Lawyers solve legal problems.
- Ministers solve spiritual problems.
- Teachers solve intellectual problems.
- Chefs solve appetite problems.

One of the greatest lessons I have learned in the arena of success is this: **The most valuable person you will ever encounter in life is a genuine problem solver.**

> THE MOST VALUABLE PERSON YOU WILL EVER ENCOUNTER IN LIFE IS A GENUINE PROBLEM SOLVER.

Every problem in life has a solution. And *you* have been designed *to be the answer to somebody's problem!* You have a valuable contribution to make; someone *needs* the answers that only you can provide. The key to your future lies in finding those people and solving those problems!

What problems are you here to solve? Choose, on purpose, to solve problems. You will create a successful outcome for your life, no matter how bad things look for you today.

When you determine to live a principle-based life, you aren't controlled by other people's wrong actions or words. Instead, you wake up every morning with a problem solver's mentality. You tell yourself: *"I am going to solve every problem that comes before me today. I'm not going to log it. I'm not going to sit around and think about it. I'm going to solve it. I'm going to look for problems to solve for people. I'm determined to make a difference in their lives."*

How does all this apply to the workplace?

Whether people smile or frown when you walk into a room is in direct proportion to the problems you solve. People either think, *"Here comes a solution,"* or they think, *"Oh, no — here comes that problem again!"* You either solve or create problems every day of your life. You cannot be neutral.

If we would sit back and evaluate our past performance at our jobs, we would likely discover that we have solved fewer problems than we thought. If you find this to be true in your case, you need to start making the needed adjustments right away. You see, the moment we create more problems than we solve, we become not only unnecessary, but detrimental to the organization. **Your value to your employer is in direct proportion to the problems you are willing to solve for him.**

> YOUR VALUE
> TO YOUR EMPLOYER IS
> IN DIRECT PROPORTION
> TO THE PROBLEMS
> YOU ARE WILLING
> TO SOLVE FOR HIM.

For instance, if a person has a chronic bad attitude in the workplace, it is only a matter of time before he is replaced. He has now lit the fatal fuse on the outcome of his position in that job. How can I say that? It's very simple. It is unnatural for a businessperson to maintain a painful relationship. The moment he finds a better way, he gets rid of the painful relationship.

So become an indispensable problem *solver* instead of a problem *creator*. Take on the tasks other people do not want, and perform your assigned tasks better than anyone else.

> YOU WILL ONLY BE
> REMEMBERED FOR THE
> PROBLEMS YOU SOLVE
> OR THE PROBLEMS
> YOU CREATE.

If you determine to become a self-motivated problem solver, you have *nowhere to go but up* in the company or business for which you work! Favor and promotion are assured the moment solving problems becomes your focus.

Part of being a *self-motivated* problem solver is that you do not need to continually *ask* your supervisor, "What is the problem I can solve for you?" If you have to constantly ask, YOU have now become the prob-

> FINANCES ARE AWARDED
> TO THE EMPLOYEE
> WHO MAKES SOLVING
> PROBLEMS HIS FOCUS.

lem! An astute problem solver works to *discover* the problems, and then solves them.

I believe the number one neglected truth in career training and business workshops today is this: **Finances are awarded to the employee who makes solving problems his focus.**

When business leaders and financial advisors teach about wealth, they need to teach about *problem solving*, because that is the means by which all wealth comes. **Money is simply the reward for solving problems.**

This is the reason millions and millions of people attend financial seminars and hear wealth-building principles week after week and still stay poor. They never learn the art of problem solving.

Once you become a problem solver, opportunity for advancement is easy. There is rarely any competition in problem solving

Everyone will think you're a fool because you constantly look for ways to serve and help the people around you. But in the end, they see that the rewards for a problem solver are promotion and prosperity!

ATTENTIVENESS:
THE KEY TO PROBLEM SOLVING

The word attentive implies a tireless choice to concentrate. To be attentive to another, you must hear and understand exactly what the other person says. To be an effective problem solver, you must demonstrate attentiveness to those around you, especially those you are assigned to serve.

- **When someone addresses you, don't allow yourself to remain preoccupied.** Put down what you are doing, face the person, make eye contact, and give them your full attention.
- **Listen to what the other person is dealing with; then help solve their problem.** As you listen, notice what they are not saying, as well as what they say.
- **If someone in authority gives you an instruction, don't be casual about it.** Be ready to do exactly what he asks of you, as soon as he finishes speaking.

I am convinced that attentiveness determines how far a person can actually go in an organization.

Attentiveness means showing the worth of a person, an object, or an idea by giving it your undivided concentration. Why is this character trait so significant? Because the outcome of our lives is not determined by the weightier matters that we think are so important. Winning or losing is in the details, the small particulars of life to which most people pay no attention.

Attentiveness implies deep concentration to details. An inattentive employee only skims over the assignment given, never taking the time to carefully look over the details. Attentive employees meticulously attend to everything their boss or supervisor asks of them. They concentrate on the details of the assignment, making sure to cover all the bases. Attentive people stand out from others. Their work is exceptional, while those who are inattentive cut corners and do a half-hearted job.

Attentiveness is closely related to excellence. Without careful attention to detail, there cannot be pursuit of excellence. In every situation you face in life, be mindful of the details. What are the little particulars that other people don't see or pay attention to? Attentive people have learned the art of listening.

EFFECTIVE LISTENING

Listening is the key to attentiveness, but how do you become an effective listener? You have to understand exactly what listening is. While hearing is a function of our ears, listening is a function of our mind. It is something we choose to do. Nobody chooses to hear — our ears work no matter what we do. But we must make a decision to listen.

> **ATTENTIVENESS IS A DAILY HABIT THAT CAUSES YOU TO FOCUS ON THAT WHICH TRULY MATTERS TO OTHERS.**

Listening is made up of two separate aspects. The first is **understanding what the speaker says.** What do they mean? It is the ability to accurately translate what they said into your own understanding. The second is the **ability to focus single-mindedly upon the one speaking,** by reading facial and body expressions.

SEVEN WAYS TO BE MORE ATTENTIVE

1. Don't just hear — listen.
Discover what is considered a job well done. Listen, so you can give your superior what he really wants.

2. Write it down.
When you write down your instructions, you show that you value what is being said, and that you will do what you are told. Don't trust your memory. It is estimated that the short-term memory will only store something for forty seconds. Always have a paper and a pen ready. Your boss will be more detailed when he sees you writing; and the more detailed his

instructions, the more excellence you can apply to fulfilling his request.

3. Interpret it back to him.

Always repeat back what you thought you heard the speaker say. You may have heard something other than what was meant. When you reiterate what was said, your boss will know you understand, or he'll correct your misunderstandings. This step will save you time in the long run.

4. Ask him to prioritize his instructions.

When given a list of things to do, ask which items are most important. Complete them in order of importance. What you think is important may not be as important to your employer.

5. Act quickly.

Get to work immediately, remembering that accuracy is more important than speed. Combine both as much as possible.

6. Report back.

Keep your boss up to date on your progress. Lack of communication breeds uncertainty. You should never have to be asked for a progress report. Make it your responsibility to communicate to your supervisor.

7. Never complain.

You may say, "I never say anything negative to my boss or my fellow employees." I commend you on that, but complaining doesn't always have to be voiced. It can be communicated by body language. How do you respond when your boss gives you an instruction? Do you smile and welcome it, or do you show that you are not happy to hear what he has to say? Your body language makes a big difference.

Effective
Listening

☑ Don't Just Hear–Listen
☑ Write It Down
☑ Reinterpret
☑ Ask For Priorities
☑ Act Quickly
☑ Report Back
☑ Never Complain

You Are Not Your Own Problem Solver

The sad truth is, most people are *not* problem *solvers*. Many have no success in this arena because they expect life to revolve around them. Their entire focus is on doing whatever it takes to get other people to solve *their* problems.

> OUR EMPLOYERS HAVE NOT BEEN APPOINTED TO SOLVE OUR PROBLEMS; WE HAVE BEEN APPOINTED TO SOLVE THEIRS.

Many great men and women have been disqualified because of their refusal to walk the road of problem solving. A person cannot be promoted unless he solves someone else's problems. **We were designed to focus on solving others' problems, not our own.**

Keep in mind that whatever help you give to others is the same help you may one day need. It boils down to this: you can't accomplish very much in your life if you don't have someone to solve problems for you. You need people who truly have a heart for your success and who desire to be what you need them to be in your life. Without these problem solvers, you go around and around the same mountain again and again, never advancing very far at all.

You are not meant to fix your own problems; there is someone out there assigned to help you. But how do you find *your* problem solvers? What do you do when you feel like no one really cares for your well-being?

The Golden Rule

The concept behind this principle *is not* a matter of "You wash my back, and I'll wash yours. You give to me, and I'll give to you." Many fearful, insecure people live their lives in "reaction mode," giving *only* to keep the ledger books balanced. They don't want to give too much, because they are stingy. And they don't want to

> NO ONE ON EARTH CAN STOP THE ADVANCEMENT OF A REAL PROBLEM SOLVER!

receive a gift because they do not want to feel obligated, accountable, or beholden to anyone.

That reminds me of a custom many people have in America when they get married. They keep a log of how much money people give them as a wedding gift. Then, if any of the people who gave them monetary gifts get married, the couple gives that *same amount* of money back to them as a gift — no more and no less!

The dynamic of The Golden Rule, however, runs much deeper than petty account keeping. It states: **"And just as you want men to do to you, you also do to them likewise."** How do you want to be treated? That is the way you should first treat others.

Even an unprincipled person understands the idea, "If you do something for me, I'll do something for you." That's the way the world does business. But a principled individual takes that idea to a much higher level by *purposefully* solving problems for others and then trusts in the power of that seed to bring a harvest of solutions for *his* problems.

No one can stop the advancemnet of a real problem solver. You have to get that fact planted deep in your heart. *No one can stop you!* People may want to set up roadblocks to keep you from moving upward, but you'll just sidestep those roadblocks and keep on rising to the next level!

Your social or economic status doesn't really matter — it doesn't matter whether you are at the top of the ladder or on the bottom rung. You *will* receive back the good things you do for others! As you solve problems for others, your prosperity and promotion will come.

It doesn't matter if people try to stand in your way. It doesn't matter if your employer disappoints you, puts you down, or even throws you out. All you need to do is maintain your commitment to integrity and continue to be a problem solver for others. *Then, whatever you make happen for others, the same will happen for you!*

PRINCIPLES OF PROMOTION

It's easy to understand why so many people go unrewarded in the workplace. They just don't do what is necessary to *be* rewarded. Although life is designed to be a continual ascension, most people are at a perpetual standstill. They simply *exist* at their jobs, doing their tasks by rote.

What is the root of their condition? Somewhere along the line, they stopped solving the problems of those to whom they were appointed.

You can't do that if you want to be promoted. You have to continually press into problem solving. You have to ask yourself constantly: *What problems can I solve for my employer today? What can I do to make his life easier?*

In fact, take it one step further — **pursue solving problems for your employer long before they become your assignment.**

> PURSUE SOLVING
> PROBLEMS LONG BEFORE
> THEY BECOME YOUR
> ASSIGNMENT.

By staying ahead of the inevitable (that is when the problem is actually assigned to you), you can make the problem work for you by solving it beforehand.

Think about it — why would you want to wait to solve a certain problem when you know that you eventually will have to deal with it anyway? So, if you see the problem coming, stay ahead of the game. Start solving that problem before it sneaks up behind you and smacks you on the head, turning your entire schedule upside down as you try to fix it.

Be sure that you are qualified to solve the problems you may recognize. Don't move before you know for certain you are able to handle any given problem.

You see, sometimes people try to solve problems at their job that simply are not theirs to fix, because it isn't in the power of their hand to do it. Or they spend all their time trying to solve problems for the unqualified, or for those to whom it is not due. Then they wonder why they do not see multiplication in their lives!

Don't become a busybody. These people tend to infect everyone else with their negative words of gossip and complaint. They incessantly want to let you know about their aches and pains or what someone else did to offend them. Whatever useless tidbit of information they have to give, the situation only worsens when you listen and sympathize.

People who waste most of their time trying to solve the problems of the unqualified do not understand a key precept: **A problem solver is good to everyone, but especially good to some.**

Exclusivity is important to a genuine problem solver. He kicks it up a notch when it comes to solving problems for the *specific people he is assigned to serve.*

When I relate to those whom I have been assigned to serve, I want to know, *"Where am I on your list of problem solvers in your life? Am I number six? Number eight? Number nine? Because if you tell me I'm number nine, you give me something to shoot for. I'll go after the goal of becoming your number one problem solver! Just bring me anything that no one else wants to do, and you'll find the task completed before the sun goes down!"*

> YOUR VALUE AS A PERSON DOES NOT COME FROM YOUR RACE, COLOR, OR CREED, BUT BY THE TYPES OF PROBLEMS YOU ARE WILLING TO SOLVE FOR OTHERS.

Here's another principle that will help you attain that higher level you seek in the workplace: **Your value as a person does not come from your race, color, or creed, but by the types of problems you are willing**

to solve for others.

The person who cleans the bathrooms may very well be a wonderful person, and I am deeply grateful for such people! Where would we be without them? But as long as cleaning bathrooms is the problem this person chooses to solve with his life, his choice determines that he will live within the means of a limited amount of finances. He won't go far beyond that level of wages until he begins to solve a higher level of problems for someone else.

> **TO RECEIVE A GREATER REWARD, ALL ONE MUST DO IS SOLVE A GREATER PROBLEM.**

One person may hold a secretarial job and earn $8.00 an hour. Another person is an attorney, and his clients pay him $300.00 an hour. Why is this? The reason is not that the secretary has less value as a person than the attorney. It is just that the attorney solves a greater problem. The type of problems a person solves for others determines the amount for which he is recompensed for his labor.

For instance, if an employee wants a raise, his employer has the right to ask him, "What new kinds of problems are you going to solve for me that warrant more money than you make right now?" That rationale makes a lot more sense than an employee who says, "Well, everyone else in the office gets a raise in January, so I want one too."

If you desire to see multiplication in your paycheck, you must first be instrumental in bringing multiplication into the business for which you work. When you help the business grow, you see your reward grow.

In other words, you will be rewarded only when you deserve it.

DON'T REJECT
THE PROBLEM SOLVERS IN YOUR LIFE

There are so few true problem solvers in the world today. I am thankful for every one of them, especially those appointed to take me to the woodshed every now and then! When these people visit me, we do not sit around exchanging small talk. We get right down to business, talking about what needs to change in my life.

It is seldom easy to sit through those conversations. There are times I come away feeling like I have just been through a meat grinder! But I wouldn't have it any other way. I want to reach the finish line to become all I am intended to be, and these problem solvers are designated to help me get there. They are concerned about my future. They know my potential, and they don't want me to remain where I am.

FINISH STRONG

You see, we don't need someone to be there for us at the beginning of the race nearly as much as we need someone at the end of the race. At the starting gate, we look good with our leg warmers and our workout outfits. But by the end of the race, we don't run in a pack with the other runners anymore; we all just straggle in one by one.

In fact, most of the runners around us in the beginning of the race never make it to the end! As I said earlier, most people are good starters, but very few are good finishers. Most of us are very good at starting project after project after project. But it seems that almost every time we get to the middle of something, we get distracted, lose interest, get bored, and quit.

Meanwhile, we just try to get our exhausted bodies across the finish line. **This is the time we make the most mistakes, if we don't have problem solvers along the sidelines, cheering us on and guiding us along the way.**

Perhaps now you can see why problem solving is the key that opens the doors of opportunity and success in any area of life, including the workplace. To live a life of continual ascension into your best life, you must not only become a problem solver for those to whom you have been assigned, but you must also embrace those who have been appointed to guide *you* along your way — even when they take you to your most difficult testing ground!

CHAPTER SEVEN SUMMARY

- You tell yourself: *"I am going to solve every problem that comes before me today. I'm not going to log it. I'm not going to sit around and think about it. I'm going to solve it. I'm going to look for problems to solve for people. I'm determined to make a difference in their lives."*

- You see, the moment we create more problems than we solve, we become not only unnecessary, but also detrimental to the organization for which we work.

- If you determine to become a self-motivated problem solver, you have nowhere to go but up in the company or business for which you work!

- Many great men and women are disqualified because of their refusal to walk the road of problem solving. A person cannot be promoted unless he solves someone else's problems.

- *No one can stop the advancement of a real problen solver.* You have to get that fact planted deep in your heart. No one can stop you! People may want to set up roadblocks to keep you from moving upward, but you'll just sidestep those roadblocks and keep on rising to the next level!

- It's easy to understand why so many people go unrewarded in the workplace. They just don't do the necessary things to be rewarded. Although life is designed to be a continual ascension, most people are at a perpetual standstill.

- So, if you see the problem coming, stay ahead of the game. Start solving that problem before it sneaks up behind you and smacks you on the head, turning your entire schedule upside down as you try to fix it.

- One person is a secretary and earns $8.00 an hour. Another person is an attorney, and his clients pay him $300.00 an hour. Why is this? The reason is not that the secretary has less value as a person than the attorney. It is just that the attorney chooses to solve a greater problem.

- There are so few true problem solvers in the world today. I am thankful for every one of them, especially those appointed to take me to the woodshed every now and then!

- To live a life of continual ascension into your best life, you must not only become a problem solver for those to whom you have been assigned, but you must also embrace those who have been appointed to guide you along your way — even when they take you to your most difficult testing ground!

PRINCIPLES FOR PROBLEM SOLVING

- Become A Person Who Chooses To Solve Problems For Others.

- What Is Done To You Never Determines The Outcome Of Your Life; It Is How You *Respond* To Injustice That Determines Your Destiny.

- Your Value To Your Employer Is In Direct Proportion To The Problems You Are Willing To Solve For Him.

- You Will Only Be Remembered For The Problems You Solve Or The Problems You Create.

- In Problem Solving, Become Indispensable By Choosing To Solve The Problems Others Refuse To Undertake.

- Never Require Oversight But Always Welcome Inspection.

- Finances Are Awarded To The Employee Who Makes Solving Problems His Focus.

- To Find Your Problem Solvers, Solve Others' Problems First.

- The Only Way You Can Tell You Are A True Problem Solver Is When Others Begin To Take Care Of *Yours*.

- No One Can Stop The Advancement Of A Real Problem Solver.

- Pursue Solving Problems For Your Employer Long Before They Become Your Assignment.

- Problem Solving Is Doing More Than You Need To, Not Because You Have To, But Because You *Want* To.

- A Problem Solver Is Good To Everyone, But Especially Good To Some.

- Your Value As A Person Does Not Come From Your Race, Color, Or Creed, But By The Types Of Problems You Are Willing To Solve For Others.

- To Receive A Greater Reward, All One Must Do Is Solve A Greater Problem.

- You Receive A Promotion When You Successfully Overcome The Problems You Are Presently Paid To Solve.

Servanthood:
The Key To Greatness

YOU MUST BECOME A SERVANT
BEFORE YOU CAN EVER QUALIFY
TO BECOME A TRUE PROBLEM SOLVER.

As I stated in the previous chapter, problem solving ushers you into favor and promotion more quickly than any other known quality — and the fastest, most efficient way to become a problem solver is to first *become a servant*. But how do you know when you truly are a servant?

Many people submit to their authorities only to avoid the negative consequences they will experience if they don't. People know that if they act contrary to their employer's wishes, their employer will enact negative consequences, such as the loss of a paycheck or actual job.

Obviously this is not the true measure of a servant. The more you enlarge your capacity to serve people with a right heart, the more you grow into greatness. You won't be controlled by fear of consequences; instead, you will serve others because it becomes a genuine inner desire.

A true servant finds his fulfillment through bringing pleasure to the one he or she serves. He becomes an extension of his employer's influence into arenas where the employer is unable to go. Most importantly, a true servant never allows offense into his or her life.

Usually, when people are treated in an ill manner, they retract their willingness to serve. They say, "I'm not going to serve you anymore because of the way you spoke to me," or "You did this to me, so I'm finished with serving you!" But, in the words of my friend, Dr. Bill Gothard: **"The true test of a servant is if he acts like one when he is treated like one."**

STRIFE-FREE WORKPLACE

You just cannot afford to take offense in the workplace. If strife and resentment begin to govern the way you relate to your employer or your co-workers, the offense could end up costing you more than you'll ever know.

> OFFENSE
> IS NEVER ALLOWED TO
> ENTER THE ATMOSPHERE
> OF A SERVANT.

People say, "Oh, I just blew up and got angry that one time. It's no big deal, but I'm sorry."

You know, sometimes "sorry" just doesn't cut it. If we are going to be people of excellence in the workplace, we must continually filter our outgoing communication. Instead of doing the damage and then afterward saying, "Oh, I'm sorry," we should be able to say, "Before I caused an argument and had a fit of anger, I decided not to do it!"

SERVE YOUR EMPLOYER WELL

Serving others has one very noticeable effect: It changes *you*. When I first started learning how to be a servant, one of my elders said to me, "I'll tell you what, Robb. You say you're a servant?"

"Yes, Sir," I answered.

"All right," he said. "Then you be here at 5:00 a.m."

I said, "Yes, Sir!" — and I was there right on time at five o'clock. The man couldn't believe it, but I was just operat-

> TRUE SERVANTHOOD
> IS MARKED BY THE
> WILLINGNESS TO
> ABANDON ALL TO BECOME
> A TOOL IN THE HAND
> OF ANOTHER.

ing within the following principle: **True servanthood is marked by the willingness to abandon all to become a tool in the hand of another.**

You may say, "But you don't know the pressures and problems I'm dealing with. How do I just unload them before I come to work and become what my employer wants me to be?"

I realize those problems may seem big to you. However, the true size of the problems you face is relative to the attitude with which you face them.

I remember a friend telling me that his little third grade sister once said to him, "You think *you* owe money (he owed thousands of dollars)! My life is over! I owe someone at school *forty-two cents!*"

Problems indeed seem big or small, depending on the perspective you have in life. So, although your problems might seem huge, each morning as you enter the workplace, make a practice of focusing on being a solution instead of on your own problems. Determine to serve well as you become what your employer needs you to be for that day.

CHARACTERISTICS OF A TRUE SERVANT

Now with all this in mind, let's talk about the characteristics of a true servant.

1. A true servant is PROVEN.

A true servant embraces the times people take him to his proving ground. This is the way to keep from becoming a casualty in the workplace. When someone leads you to your testing ground, don't run from the situation. Instead, *embrace* it as an opportunity to pass another test and prove yourself. **The genuine servant welcomes the opportunity to prove his authenticity.**

> THE GENUINE SERVANT WELCOMES THE OPPORTUNITY TO PROVE HIS AUTHENTICITY.

Sometimes it's difficult to recognize when someone is leading you to your testing ground. You just think people are invading your life in a way they have no right to. You may think the requests being made of you are greater than anything that should ever be asked of any person. You may even think, "How dare my employer ask me to do that! I know I wanted to be a servant, but I never thought it would require me to do this!"

I know of several prominent individuals who never made it through their testing ground — and no one has heard of them since. They faded into obscurity, because they refused to maintain a servant's heart.

You must understand: **In careful examination of the proving grounds of life, you discover that *the valleys of testing are also the mountains of rewards*.**

Personally, I *want* to be taken to my proving ground. I look forward to the test that takes me to the next level. I want to be taken to a place where someone I respect sits me down and says, "Now, you really need to take care of this responsibility," or "You really need to make this change."

I recall a time recently when one of my mentors began to set the stage for a serious discussion. When I discovered what he was doing, I politely interrupted him and said, "Respectfully, Sir, you don't have to beat around the bush. Please tell me exactly what you want me to do, and it will be done before the sun goes down." It would not even matter to me if that individual did not care for me, for I will never allow someone's disregard of me to stand in the way of my promotion.

> IN CAREFUL EXAMINATION OF THE PROVING GROUNDS OF LIFE, YOU DISCOVER THAT THE VALLEYS OF TESTING ARE ALSO THE MOUNTAINS OF REWARDS.

Developing a servant's heart is not a game, and it is not for the faint-hearted or the easily offended. Think about it — people around the world today are losing their lives by taking a stand for what is right. Yet, many employees get offended simply because they don't like it when their employer asks them to do something they don't want to do!

You may as well get ready, because you will be tested in your character on your way to becoming a true servant. Otherwise, you will never be able to be trusted with higher responsibility.

2. A true servant is DILIGENT.

A proverb states, *"He who has a slack hand becomes poor, but the hand of the diligent makes rich."* You see, in order to become all that you were intended to become, you need a substantial amount of finances. Money is necessary to fulfill your divine purpose in life. However, you have to go about obtaining that wealth *the right way* — the way of diligence.

To maintain a diligent attitude at work, always focus on this question: *"What benefit does my employer receive from his relationship with me?"* That kind of attitude will reap a great harvest for you that can never be obtained by asking, *"What am I getting out of all this hard work I'm doing for my employer?"*

3. A true servant is FAITHFUL.

We have already talked about this quality in a previous chapter. But let me stress this point: **You are not to be faithful according to the standards you set for yourself. Faithfulness is defined by the standards of the one you are assigned to serve.**

> IN LIFE, WE MUST NOT STRIVE FOR THE ABILITY TO TAKE CRITICISM, BUT RATHER PURSUE THE ABILITY TO RECEIVE INSTRUCTION.

Our faithfulness is not judged according to others' standards; our faithfulness is judged according to the standards of those who have been placed over us.

That is why you should follow this guideline: *Never take an instruction from a person who is unable to give you a promotion.* Identify the one who can promote you, and then be willing to receive instruction.

Why must we learn to receive instruction? Because that is the only way we will be counted faithful by the standards of those in authority over us. When we consistently receive and act on our authority's instructions, we don't have to keep taking correction for the same mistake again and again. Instruction received and acted upon prevents the next time of correction.

Remain teachable; otherwise you won't be able to receive your supervisor's correction. Refuse to guard and protect yourself when he gives you correction or instruction. **Your superior cannot help you grow or improve until you become teachable.**

Some people never learn from their mistakes, nor do they ever learn how to receive the instruction they need to change. In order to walk in the promotion you desire, you must change and continue to grow.

That only happens when you assume a posture of one who welcomes instruction. We don't ever have to remain where we are. If we don't like the results with which we live today, we need only change our actions. Thus, whatever we do not like, we can change.

Now, I'm a quick learner. All you need to do is show me what I am doing wrong. Just show me my "PRD" — my "Position Results Description" — that tells me, "This job will be completed when you have successfully accomplished the following tasks." I'll leave with my assignment and come back to you with a successfully completed job!

> PROMOTIONS ARE THE REWARDS YOU RECEIVE THE MOMENT YOU STAND HEAD AND SHOULDERS ABOVE OTHERS IN THE EYES OF YOUR SUPERIORS.

At the end of my life, I do not want to look back and wish that I had received instruction better, so that the outcome of my time on this earth would be different.

Let's look at the final characteristic of servanthood — an important attribute that we have already discussed at length.

4. A true servant is RESPECTFUL.

As we previously discussed, a servant is *respectful*. Everything about him, from the tone of his voice to his body language, conveys honor and respect for his superior. This respect is *genuine*, not simply an artificial show that disappears when his superior no longer watches.

You are not to give your employer a half-hearted form of respect. You are not to speak one way in front of him and another way behind his back. *Full* respect means a 360-degree type of respect that is given 24 hours a day, 7 days a week!

The most evident expression of respect or disrespect is in your actions and words. **It is impossible for your life to go in a different direction than your present actions.**

However, don't dwell on the wrong words and actions of days gone by. You can't keep digging up your past if you want to go on to a higher level. As a

> THE SECRET OF YOUR FUTURE IS HIDDEN IN THE ACTIONS OF TODAY.

servant, you have to let go of your past mistakes and failures. Otherwise, those mistakes take you through a meteor shower of disappointment and distraction; they keep you from achieving the success that awaits you in the days ahead.

CHARACTERISTICS OF A FALSE SERVANT

With every truth, there comes a counterfeit. With genuine servant-hood, there also comes false servanthood. Let's look at a few character-istics of false servants.

1. A false servant is IDLE.

A false servant is a person who does not fulfill his basic responsibilities. On the job, his work area is unkempt and disorganized. He spends too much time around the water cooler chatting with co-workers, and not enough time doing what he is supposed to do!

This person fits the description of the bad servant spoken of by this proverb: *"He also that is slothful in his work is brother to him that is a great waster."*

It becomes very frustrating for an employer to deal with a person like this. He finds himself continually lowering his standards, just to avoid an argument with the lazy employee.

Put plainly, idleness is theft and disrespect. An idle servant steals time and money from his employer. He disrespects not only his employer, but also himself; and one cannot progress if he has no respect for himself.

2. A false servant is DISHONEST.

The Bible tells us, *"Whoever can be trusted with very little can also be trusted with much…"* That's a good principle to remember the next time you are tempted to talk on the telephone with a friend during compa-ny time or take home some pens and paperclips from the office for your own personal use!

If a person isn't an honest and a trustworthy servant in the little things, he won't be trusted with the big things. Dishonesty is a big reason many people never rise to the next level in the workplace.

3. A false servant is DISLOYAL.

Disloyalty is a horrible thing. It is a cancer to workplace excellence. Inasmuch as it hurts an employer or a mentor, it hurts the unfaithful person even more. *Disloyalty disqualifies you from rising to the apex of your career or occupation.*

4. A false servant is ARGUMENTATIVE.

A false servant is contentious and over-opinionated. Your employer does not desire your opinions — he wants your productivity! You must never allow your speech to become careless regarding any authority figure. Strife and combativeness are some of the highest forms of insubordination. They stop your promotion.

A FALSE SERVANT
CAN CHANGE FOR THE BETTER

It truly doesn't matter where you are right now in your job. It doesn't matter if you are currently disqualified from being called a true servant. Just remember — you can *re-qualify*. And how do you do that? *Simply make things right with your authorities.* The doors of opportunity are reopened by becoming first a true servant and then a problem solver. This is how we enjoy genuine promotion.

I am thankful that I determined never to quit in the areas of my life where I had once disqualified myself. I never said it was too late to keep trying; I never threw in the towel. Says David T. Scoates, *"It's always too soon to quit!"*

When qualified authority spoke words of correction into my life, I never for a moment accused them of being wrong. I just kept pursuing excellence, until I re-qualified myself for true servanthood.

Be encouraged by the words of B.C. Forbes: *"History has demonstrated that the most notable winners usually encountered heartbreaking obstacles before they triumphed. They won because they refused to become discouraged by their defeats."*

If you are going to receive the promotions in store for you, that has to be your determination. If you refuse to give up — if you keep on going until every hindrance is uncovered and destroyed — *nothing* can stand in the way of your becoming all you were created to become!

You Choose
Your Own Consequences

This is my continual affirmation: *"I cannot be stopped. I will succeed!"* I simply will not allow anything to get in the way of my pursuit toward excellence. I make this my guiding principle in life: **The harvest of your future is hidden in your choices of today.**

It's one thing to make a mistake. It's another to make a wrong choice. Mistakes can be forgiven, but we must live with the consequences of our choices.

> THE HARVEST OF YOUR FUTURE IS HIDDEN IN YOUR CHOICES OF TODAY.

Consider this: More than ninety percent of the people with whom you work every day do not like their job. Consequently, they have a poor attitude, and really have no idea what it means to have a servant's heart. All they want to do is get someone to listen to their long list of complaints, which usually includes the following:

- *They are always "misunderstood" for some reason.*
- *They are under-compensated.*
- *No one encourages or edifies them on the job.*
- *They never receive any benefit from their job — and it's entirely their employer's fault.*

I don't believe any of these statements hold true. Everyone has a free will, so why do these people allow their lives and their attitudes to be determined by someone else at their jobs? Why should other people determine whether or not they're happy with their work?

The truth is, the outcome of our lives is based on the decisions *we* make. We choose our own consequences. We cannot blame our unhappiness or our bad attitudes on others.

I no longer think only from the perspective of whether or not a decision is right or wrong. Now, I always take the time to evaluate what kind of *consequences* will result from the decision I am about to make. Before any decision, answer this question, *"What is going to happen if I do this?"*

To become a person of excellence, train yourself to think this way. Live with a long-term perspective. In other words, **choose to pay the price now to enjoy the greatest benefits later. Embrace the short-term pain in order to enjoy long-term pleasure.**

When we make a major decision that gives us nothing but immediate, short-term gratification, we will likely pay for that decision for the rest of our lives. One wrong decision could start us down a road that leaves us marred and scarred in the end.

That is why it is so important for us to understand that our lives are completely determined by the choices we make; each decision has a predetermined outcome. For instance, suppose we get up tomorrow morning and decide we don't want to do a good job at work that day. That is our choice — but we better be ready for our employer to say,

"You need to pick up your severance check because we don't need you anymore!" We shouldn't wonder, "Why did this happen to me?"

Recently, a young business owner expressed to me how thankful she was for my input into her new business. However, she told me she was dealing with one particular challenge: With all the new business that was coming in, she was having a difficult time focusing.

I responded with these words: "Don't even think about it. If you don't find the resolve to focus on your new business, it won't be long before you won't have to deal with that challenge anymore, because the new business will stop coming in!"

I was just letting this business owner know what we all need to understand: The outcome of her business endeavor depends on whether or not she embraces short-term pain in order to enjoy long-term pleasure.

Charles A. Lindbergh, Jr. pointed out, *"Success is not measured by what a man accomplishes, but by the opposition he has encountered, and the courage with which he maintained the struggle against overwhelming odds."* Embrace the pain — and then be grateful for the gain.

CHAPTER EIGHT SUMMARY

- The more you enlarge your capacity to serve people with a right heart the more you will grow into greatness.

- Serving others has one very noticeable effect: it changes you.

- So, although your problems might seem huge, each morning as you enter the workplace make a practice of focusing on being a solution instead of on your own problems. Determine to serve well as you become what your employer needs you to be for that day.

- People around the world today are losing their lives by taking a stand for what is right. Yet, many employees get offended simply because they don't like it when their employer asks them to do something they don't want to do!

- Refuse to guard and protect yourself when he gives you correction or instruction. Your superior cannot help you grow or improve until you become teachable.

- At the end of my life, I do not want to look back and wish that I had received instruction better, so that the outcome of my time on this earth would have been different.

- With every truth, there comes a counterfeit. With genuine servanthood, there also comes false servanthood.

- An idle servant steals time and money from his employer. He disrespects not only his employer, but also himself; and one cannot progress if he has no respect for himself.

- B.C. Forbes: *"History has demonstrated that the most notable winners usually encountered heartbreaking obstacles before they triumphed. They won because they refused to become discouraged by their defeats."*

- Consider this: more than ninety percent of the people with whom you work every day do not like their job. Consequently, they have a poor attitude, and really have no idea what it means to have a servant's heart.

- Charles A. Lindbergh, Jr. pointed out, *"Success is not measured by what a man accomplishes, but by the opposition he has encountered, and the courage with which he maintained the struggle against overwhelming odds."*

PRINCIPLES FOR SERVANTHOOD

- You Must Become A Servant Long Before You Ever Become A Trusted Problem Solver.

- The Litmus Test Of A Servant Is If He Acts Like One When He Is Treated Like One.

- Offense Is Never Allowed To Enter The Atmosphere Of A Servant.

- True Servanthood Is Marked By The Willingness To Abandon All To Become A Tool In The Hand Of Another.

- The Genuine Servant Welcomes The Opportunity To Prove His Authenticity.

- In Careful Examination Of The Proving Grounds Of Life You Discover That The Valleys Of Testing Are Also The Mountains Of Reward.

- Faithfulness To One's Own Standards Profit Little. Faithfulness Is Defined By The Standards Of Those To Whom You Have Been Assigned.

- Never Take An Instruction From A Person Who Is Unable To Give You A Promotion.

- In Life, We Must Not Strive For The Ability To Take Criticism, But Rather Pursue The Ability To Receive Instruction.

- Promotions Are The Rewards You Receive The Moment You Stand Head And Shoulders Above Others In The Eyes Of Your Superiors.

- The Secret Of Your Future Is Hidden In The Actions Of Today.

- The Harvest Of Your Future Is Hidden In Your Choices Of Today.

Ethics:
The Difference
All Men Are Looking For

INTEGRITY IS THE FOUNDATION UPON
WHICH YOUR LIFE'S WORK IS BUILT.

The high morals and values that past generation parents once instilled into their children are rarely taught today. Because many children grow up without a strong ethical foundation, they don't know what is right or wrong. They grow into adulthood thinking low standards, such as lying, cheating, and manipulating others, are acceptable. Unknown to them, their lives are on a collision course with failure.

However, lately I have noticed that this issue of strong ethics in the workplace is becoming increasingly important. Something has begun to change in our society. Employers are beginning to look for people of integrity, people who have purpose and who pursue excellence in their jobs.

The word "ethics" refers to a *person's manners or morals*. Ethics can be said to *provide a system of principles or a set of values that teaches people their duty, and rules their lives in every situation, even when no one else is watching*. Ethics can also be called *a code of conduct that governs the way a person treats others*.

An ethical person is one who understands *protocol*. In every relationship, he understands who he is, and more importantly, *who he is not*. He knows how to correctly posture himself, and does not allow himself to trespass the boundaries of honor and respect toward others, especially his superiors.

An ethical person is a person of high moral character, displayed by the way he treats others, whether it's his boss, his co-worker, or his employee. His integrity is flawless, *especially* when no one is looking.

Epictetus once said, "*A man that seeks truth and loves it must be reckoned precious to any human society.*" Likewise, a man of truth and integrity is reckoned as valuable and essential within the workplace.

Just out of the Naval Academy and flight school, Admiral Lawson was assigned the job of training officer at his first squadron. He discovered that many of his people hadn't completed required classes and that a major inspection was on the horizon. His department head, the man whose performance evaluations would affect his career, then informed him of the "standard" way these things were handled. "Go ahead and make up phony records," he said. "Take two or three different colored pens; put your X's on there; smudge up the marks a bit so the records look old; and it'll look real."

Admiral Lawson wasn't anxious to start his military career by antagonizing his superior officer, but sacrificing his integrity wasn't an option. He pledged to do a great job getting everything up to date, but he made the decision that he wasn't going to fabricate the records. Fortunately, the officer backed off. Although did take a hit on the inspection, it wasn't serious.[2]

He learned the valuable lesson that one could live up to high principles and survive.

INTEGRITY WITHOUT EXCEPTION

It is so important to conduct yourself as a person of impeccable integrity, no matter what problem or challenge you face in your business dealings or workplace. **At all times, strive to exceed the level of expectations of those above you.**

Be slow to give your word; be quick to keep it! Regardless of the circumstances, never forget that **your word is an extension of your life. Therefore, you must under-promise and over-perform.**

> YOUR WORD IS AN EXTENSION OF YOUR LIFE. THEREFORE, YOU MUST UNDER-PROMISE AND OVER-PERFORM.

Most people do the opposite! Always attempt to complete the job faster than what is expected. Compete with your own promise, and attempt to beat the finish date that you gave your customer or employer!

To be a person of excellence in the business world, you need to demonstrate keeping your word, no matter what. Refuse to compromise your word for anyone or anything.

I determined long ago that I would never knowingly break my word. After all, I have to go home with my conscience every night!

Don't ever allow an exception to your integrity, even at the risk of financial loss. Choose to lose the money, but hold on to your integrity. You will come out better in the long run.

> A PERSON OF INTEGRITY REFUSES TO ALLOW THEIR PRINCIPLES TO BE COMPROMISED.

This is admittedly a high standard, but it is the level of honesty that is expected if you desire promotion. Refuse to allow a lapse in your integrity. Thus, your consistent honesty and integrity encourage your workmates and superiors to put their trust in you.

John F. Dodge confirms: *"There is no twilight zone of honesty in business. A thing is right or it's wrong. It's black or it's white."* Perhaps now you can see why the prerequisite to become prosperous in your business or find favor at your place of employment is that you are true to yourself as well as truthful to others.

Just imagine for a moment attaining a degree of success, but knowing that you did not attain it ethically. **I would rather not attain success in the world's eyes but keep my integrity than lose my integrity for some extra cash.**

PURSUING DISTINCTION

Once you understand the importance of maintaining your integrity, it tends to draw out of you a desire for excellence. You begin to work at a higher standard of ethics than your co-workers. You understand that being of high moral character is a great advantage to you — it's a *difference* that sets you apart and distinguishes you from most other people. **It is impossible to be rewarded for your similarities to others. Rewards are reserved only for those who celebrate their difference from others.**

> IT IS IMPOSSIBLE TO BE REWARDED FOR YOUR SIMILARITIES TO OTHERS. REWARDS ARE RESERVED ONLY FOR THOSE WHO CELEBRATE THEIR DIFFERENCE FROM OTHERS.

No one chooses to drive a Ford car because it reminds them of a Chevy. I don't decide to eat at McDonald's because it reminds me of Burger King. Likewise, you are rewarded for what makes you *different* from other people, *not your similarities to them.*

The more similar you are to others, the less you'll be rewarded. So, instead of competing with others, focus on what makes you *uniquely different.* Do what others are *unwilling to do.* Present yourself in such a way that you excel where no one else is involved; the result will be that *you will add greater value than most.*

> EXCELLENCE
> IS NO MORE THAN THE
> PASSIONATE PURSUIT
> OF DISTINCTION.

Once you see the doors of favor open because of your differences, you never again try to be like someone else. You realize that you no longer need to be stuck in the middle of the pack, and that your excellent attitude causes you to be noticed and sought after. You can graciously say, "I do not compete with you — I *complete* you."

In what areas do you shine? What causes others to gravitate in your direction? Has your excellence set you apart as distinct, uncommon, and notable in your place of employment? I like to define excellence as this: **Excellence is no more than the passionate pursuit of distinction.**

Here are some distinctive characteristics of those who pursue excellence. The excellent:

- Stay one step ahead of the ordinary — in the workplace, this could be something as simple as getting to work early or staying longer.
- Are not satisfied with "just-good-enough" — they know that in real life, it really never is!
- Understand that today's excellence is tomorrow's mediocrity.
- Do something common in an uncommon way.
- Do their absolute best in every circumstance.
- Go beyond the status quo.

> MEDIOCRITY IS THE
> WILLINGNESS TO ACCEPT
> THE ORDINARY BECAUSE
> OF AN UNWILLINGNESS
> TO STAND FOR THE
> EXTRAORDINARY.

Mediocrity is the opposite of excellence. The mediocre:

- Deliver a second-class performance or product.

- Are happy with "just-good-enough."
- Are frail and inadequate.
- Are substandard and inferior.
- Are commonplace and ordinary.

If you desire a greater level of reward and promotion at your place of employment, avoid comfort and mediocrity as if they are poison. Demonstrate to your supervisors that you are not an ordinary employee but rather an uncommon asset with impeccable character and a strong work ethic.

A STRONG WORK ETHIC

Having a strong work ethic is not limited to being a hard worker. It includes something as simple as being courteous to the people with whom you work.

> A STRONG WORK ETHIC IS THE CATALYST THAT CAUSES OTHERS TO REWARD YOU.

We live in a world that has largely forsaken *courtesy*. A courteous person isn't interested in just spewing out his negative feelings. He actually wants to resolve issues that cause him to feel that way, so he thinks about the consequences of his words before he speaks. Will his words degrade you or cause you to lose self-esteem? Will his comments leave you worse off when you part company?

This is just a matter of courtesy, and it is the way you need to operate in your interactions with people in the workplace. Before you try to resolve a disagreement with a co-worker, consider the consequences of your words. Graciously suggest ways to fix what needs to be fixed without becoming critical and negative.

A strong work ethic also includes a constant commitment to *fulfill your responsibilities and duties on the job.*

We grew up in a generation of people who do not take personal responsibility.

> AN ETHICAL PERSON
> ALWAYS PRIZES PRINCIPLE
> ABOVE RELATIONSHIPS.

We all would prefer to live by our emotions. But there is a big problem with that. Emotions are unstable and often unpredictable; a life built around them will be unstable as well. **An ethical person always prizes principle above relationships.**

I click into operating solely by principle the moment I become unsure of what to feel about a situation. It's a place of safety for me, because principles do not change. Obeying them always creates security and desired dividends.

BE THE KIND OF PERSON THAT SETS YOU APART

Following are five qualities that when embraced bring immediate attention from your supervisors in your workplace.

1. Be an inviting person.

Learn how to plant a magnet within your heart that draws people to you and says, "I can help you." Be approachable. Wherever you go, set an atmosphere of non-judgment in which people feel free to be themselves. You can do this through a smile, or by approaching others rather than waiting for them to approach you.

2. Be a pleasing person.

People have the idea that it's unwise or demeaning to try to please

> A PLEASING DISPOSITION
> IS MAGNETIC, DRAWING
> ALL THOSE WHO COME
> IN CONTACT WITH IT.

others. People say, "I'm not a man-pleaser!" The truth is, you have to be a pleaser of men in order to get anywhere in your career. Pleasing someone other than yourself has to be your primary motive for going to work; otherwise, you won't be able to maintain a good attitude, which is so necessary to attain promotion.

No matter how much the world makes fun of you for being a man-pleaser, keep this in mind: **a pleasing disposition is magnetic, drawing all those who come in contact with it.**

You might complain, "My employer never communicates with me!" If your employer knows he has an argument on his hands every time he enters your workspace, do you think he'll keep coming in there?

I mean, even a cow is smarter than that! If you hit a cow with a two-by-four every time it walks in the barn, that old cow will stop coming to the barn! Employers gravitate toward employees who seek to please them, not toward complainers or those who constantly think they are entitled to more. **Promotions come when we pursue pleasing our employer, and we stop attempting to please our co-workers.**

We spend way too much time trying to please the people with whom we work, instead of those in authority over us. Concentrate on pleasing the one to whom you've been assigned, so that when you walk in the room, he pushes through the crowd to find you!

This won't happen because of your great personality or even the creative ideas you bring to the table. Your employer is not interested in what you think; he's interested in what *he* thinks.

> FOCUS YOUR EFFORTS
> ON WHAT YOUR EMPLOYER
> SEES, FOR THEREIN LIES
> YOUR DESTINY.

Center your attention and your problem solving skills on what *your employer* thinks, sees, feels, gets frustrated about, gets happy about, and so forth. You will immediately have his attention and gain his favor. He knows he has found an answer to his problems! First, you solve a problem, *and then* you get the position. (In today's society, most people want the position first, and then the employer is left wondering whether or not they can actually solve the problem!)

3. Be a respectful person.

Before I go any further here, I want to clarify what I mean when I use the term "respect." Respect has to do with the way we treat our superiors at work. *Ethical* people respect others both *inwardly* and *outwardly*. **To truly respect someone requires our attitude and our thoughts as well as our actions, because true respect is not just an outward posture; true respect comes from the heart.**

I have been appointed to certain people to help them succeed. These people are also in my life to prepare me for promotion. I refuse to bring one

> FORWARD PROGRESS IS FROZEN THE MOMENT YOU DEMAND YOUR OWN WAY.

second of displeasure into their lives. I will not dishonor them by falsely respecting them on the outside, while secretly disrespecting them on the inside. I will not disrespect them by pushing to do things *my way*.

If we just keep trying to work out things according to what *we* want, we never do anything except move sideways. Eventually, we might get what we want, but we never move forward or maximize our potential in the workplace.

A person of high ethics and values looks for ways to benefit *others first*, rather than insisting upon his own way. He knows that as he focuses on pleasing his authorities, his forward progress is assured.

When you pursue pleasing your authorities with singleness of purpose, you set the stage for increase to enter your life.

Someone may say, "Yes, but what should I do if my employer treats me wrongly?"

> At Any Given Moment,
> You Are Either In
> A Season Of Testing
> For Promotion Or
> A Season Of Reward
> For Accomplishments.

Realize that you are not alone, and it is not a unique situation. Each of us, at some point, finds ourselves being treated unfairly. **At any given moment you are either in a season of testing for promotion or a season of reward for accomplishments.**

You must *endure* your season of testing. Tests are a good thing — they give you the chance to *demonstrate* what you have learned. Keep in mind that diplomas are not handed out on registration day and **medals are never given out at the starting line!**

Remember, the test of whether or not you are a true servant is if you act like a servant when you are treated like one. An ethical employee passes that crucial test, and his reward surely comes!

This reminds me of another principle that is important if you are going to stand out in the crowd as a pleasing individual at your workplace: **Life must be lived from the inside out, never from the outside in.**

Many of us have been taught that it is all right to lie and to live in deception. We believe it's perfectly normal to live "in the way of eye service," acting one way when our authorities watch us and talking against them when their backs are turned.

Don't live a double life. Live your life from your heart. Your service to your supervisor has to come from the inside of you. You need to have the same attitudes about your employer on the *inside* of you that you show on the *outside*. This is the truest definition of *integrity*; it's the *"through and through-ness"* of an object or a person.

Just see what happens when you start going to work every day feeling absolutely passionate about your job. Instead of simply putting in your time, start finding ways to improve your productivity.

By the way, this is how you put yourself in a position to make more money. Just begin to be concerned about how your employer spends his business dollars. He is used to being the only person who thinks about productivity. The day you start sharing his concerns is the day you set yourself apart from the crowd in his eyes!

Think about it — how many people can you think of in your workplace that are passionate about their job and eager to please their authorities? Not many, I would imagine. Your employer could probably slash the number of his employees in half if he could just find more people who tell him, "I'm eager to serve you, and I'm here to get *you* a promotion!"

These are the kinds of people an employer doesn't have to constantly watch to make sure they do a good job.

> ANYTHING ATTEMPTED
> AND NEVER COMPLETED
> IS A PICTURE OF YOUR
> DETERMINATION.

They leave their family problems at home. They understand this principle: **Anything attempted and never completed is a picture of your determination.**

Do you mope around on the job, or are you excited about your position and the responsibilities you get to fulfill? Your approach to life is determined by your character and internal fortitude.

4. Be a compliant person.

Nine out of ten employees speak negatively concerning their employers at one time or another. I often wonder why people so readily bite the hand that feeds them.

Many times an employer feels like he is pulling teeth just to get his employees to do what he asks. He might spend thirty minutes explaining to an employee why he wants that person to follow his instructions on a particular task. But in the end, the question still comes up: "But why do I have to do it this way?"

So the employer spends another thirty minutes explaining why he, as the one in charge, thinks he made the right choice. At the end of the explanation, the employee responds, "Well, I just want you to understand the downside of what you're asking me to do." After a few replays of this scenario, that particular employee is ripe for relocation!

Don't ever make your employer *qualify* to instruct you or explain his position to you. Do not make him feel like he is pulling teeth just to get you to follow his instructions. Remember — if a person is a compliant worker, employers come looking for him. He is in great demand!

So, no matter what anyone else says or does, just keep doing your best to please your employer. Maintain the attitude, "I want to move up to the next level. No matter where I am in life, it's only temporary. There is another level and another promotion for me — *and I'm going to attain it!*"

5. Be a person with pure motives.

Nothing sets you apart more than living with a pure motive. Here is the attitude we are to carry into the workplace every day —"I'm here to promote my employer. That's my entire focus."

We are to maintain that pleasing attitude not for any selfish motives but from a pure heart. **Your motive is the key!** *Why* are you so pleasing? Is your motive to add or to extract value?

Your employer may not immediately discern your motives, but sooner or later he will. Selfish motives cannot remain hidden for long.

If your *motives are pure*, your employer will recognize it. Soon you will see doors of opportunity and favor opening. Your integrity and sincere desire to please set you apart from the crowd.

1. Respectful   2. Pleasing

Set Apart

5. Pure Motive   3. Compliant

4. Inviting

THE PRIZE OF CHARACTER

I believe many employers intuitively know the truth of this next principle, even though they may not vocalize it to their employees: **It is impossible to produce anything beyond the strength of your moral fiber.**

Character is the driving force behind all effective production and problem solving. Employers yearn for excellent work; that only comes from employees with excellent character!

> IT IS IMPOSSIBLE TO PRODUCE ANYTHING BEYOND THE STRENGTH OF YOUR MORAL FIBER.

If you are a *finisher* who conducts his affairs with strict personal *integrity*, then you are every employer's dream. Favor and promotion will surely come your way.

But you must be willing to go through present pain for future pleasure. Be willing to bow your knee today, realizing that you *will* receive a great promotion tomorrow.

ETHICAL ADVANTAGE

It has been argued that being a person of ethics and integrity puts you at a *disadvantage* in today's business world. Those who take this position are blind to both the pragmatic and eternal ramifications of their viewpoint.

Any unethical action can be made to look advantageous in the short term. A *wise* individual, however, embraces the *long-term* consequences and rewards of honesty, and thus commits to impeccable integrity and ethics within the workplace.

CHAPTER NINE SUMMARY

- The word "ethics" refers to a person's manners or morals. Ethics can be said to provide a system of principles or a set of values that teach people their duty, and rule their lives in every situation, even when no one else is watching.

- Epictetus once said, *"A man that seeks truth and loves it must be reckoned precious to any human society."*

- Don't ever allow an exception to your integrity, even at the risk of financial loss. Choose to lose the money, but hold on to your integrity. You will come out better in the long run.

- John F. Dodge confirms: *"There is no twilight zone of honesty in business. A thing is right or it's wrong. It's black or it's white."*

- Likewise, you are rewarded for what makes you different from other people, not your similarities to them.

- A courteous person isn't interested in just spewing out his negative feelings. He actually wants to resolve issues that cause him to feel that way, so he thinks about the consequences of his words before he speaks.

- Learn how to plant a magnet within your heart that draws people to you and says, "I can help you." Be approachable.

- Pleasing someone other than yourself has to be your primary motive for going to work; otherwise, you are not able to maintain a good attitude, which is so necessary to pursue excellence at your job.

- Keep in mind that diplomas are not handed out on registration day. Prizes are never given out at the starting line!

- Maintain the attitude, "I want to move up to the next level. No matter where I am in life, it's only temporary. There is another level and another promotion for me — *and I'm going to attain it!*"

- If your motives are pure, your employer will recognize it. Soon you will see doors of opportunity and favor opening.

- Character is the driving force behind all effective production and problem solving.

PRINCIPLES FOR ETHICS

→ Integrity Is The Foundation Upon Which Your Life's Work Is Built.

→ Your Word Is An Extension Of Your Life. Therefore, You Must Under-Promise And Over-Perform.

→ A Person Of Integrity Refuses To Allow Their Principles To Be Compromised.

→ It Is Impossible To Be Rewarded For Your Similarities To Others, Rewards Are Reserved Only For Those Who Celebrate Their Differences From Others.

→ Excellence Is No More Than The Passionate Pursuit Of Distinction.

→ Mediocrity Is The Willingness To Accept The Ordinary Because Of An Unwillingness To Stand For The Extraordinary.

→ A Strong Work Ethic Is The Catalyst That Causes Others To Reward You.

→ An Ethical Person Always Prizes Principle Above Relationships.

→ A Pleasing Disposition Is Magnetic, Drawing All Those Who Come In Contact With It.

→ Pleasing Your Employer, And Not Your Peers, Is An Integral Step Toward Promotion.

→ Focus Your Efforts On What Your Employer Sees, For Therein Lies Your Destiny.

→ At Any Given Moment, You Are Either In A Season Of Testing For Promotion Or A Season Of Reward For Accomplishments.

→ Diplomas Are Never Awarded On Registration Day.

→ Life Must Be Lived From The Inside Out, Never From The Outside In.

→ It Is Impossible To Produce Anything Beyond The Strength Of Your Moral Fiber.

→ The Prize Of Character Is Always Greater Than The Price Of Adversity.

Attitude:
The Heart Of Success

TO EXPERIENCE SUCCESS,
YOU MUST BECOME A MASTER OF
THE 'WIN-WIN' ATTITUDE.

In years past, the corporate world asked for people with refined skills and work experience. However, the rules have changed. Employers now focus on recruiting employees with positive attitudes, retaining them, and motivating them to perform at their maximum potential.

Those in top organizations around the globe agree that people with positive attitudes are overall better employees than those that are more qualified. A Fortune 500 study found that ninety-four percent of all the executives surveyed attributed their success to attitude more than any other factor. Why is that? Because a positive individual sees every obstacle, negative circumstance, and challenge as an opportunity to learn and grow in order to fulfill their potential. Positive people have the ability to use contrary circumstances to create the future they desire. This attitude carries over into other employees and has a great affect on the organization.

Supervior no longer tolerate negative attitudes for the sake of high qualifications. The damage caused by a negative attitude far outweighs the results from their work. There's been a complete paradigm shift. Employers no longer look for the most competent. They want those who can handle the changes, obstacles, and difficult people with a positive attitude. Consequently, you are not promoted because you are more skilled than others. **You are promoted because of the attitude you express toward your boss, co-workers, and responsibilities.**

THE DIFFERENCE YOUR ATTITUDE MAKES

You will never be remembered or rewarded for your similarities to others. You will only be rewarded because of your difference. *What makes you different?* Is it your attitude? Your difference gets you noticed by those who can promote you, and nothing will get you noticed more quickly than an excellent attitude.

You are hired primarily because of your skill, and you're promoted because of your attitude. If ninety-five percent of all employers value attitude above competence, what would you guess is the leading factor in firing? You're right! A negative attitude!

A boss doesn't mind having to train someone. What he minds is the attitude with which he must deal. Negative people are not worth employing, much less training. By simply being positive you set yourself at the top of the pool of employees because so few individuals remain positive on a consistent basis. Some might say that attitude is optional in the workplace. Yes, completing your tasks is a must, but work is a lot more fun and a lot less stressful if you have a positive attitude. Besides, negative attitudes are expressed in the quality of a person's work.

The truth, is everything won't go the way you planned. You won't get everything you want at your place of employment. No one does, not even the boss. If you remain happy and willing when plans crumble, your boss will remember you when he looks for someone to promote. Thomas Jefferson said, *"Nothing can stop the man with the right mental attitude from achieving his goal; nothing on earth can help the man with the wrong mental attitude."*

Here are five keys to sustain an excellent attitude.

1. Be willing to grow.

The only way to grow is to embrace positive change. Without change, there is no growth. Have you ever wondered why success is attracted to some people and not others? Those who are promoted constantly strive to do better.

Always posture as one who is eager to learn. Your boss knows things you don't know. Other employees know things you don't know. You can learn from them. Ask questions, make obser-

> YOUR ATTITUDE IS MAGNETIC; IT ATTRACTS OR REPELS PROMOTION.

vations, and invite critiques. Inspection and advice are to be welcomed. Ask your boss, "How can I be a better employee?" You must be sincere about changing because you might hear some things you don't like.

Consistency of attitude matters to your boss. It will take time before people believe you are genuinely interested in change. Nonetheless, change anyway.

2. Concentrate on the good.

There is good in every situation. If you look for it, you will find it. Whether it is a lesson learned, an experience shared, or a relationship built, there is always some good. Find it and enjoy it.

3. Learn from every situation.

Difficult circumstances take on a completely new meaning when you discover the hidden lesson. Whatever situation you face now needs to happen in order for you to learn an important lesson. Glean from the tough times and you will become stronger because of them.

4. Focus on the future.

Whatever challenges stand before you today, look to the future. You cannot change the past, so focus on where you desire to be and how you can get there from here. How do you want it to be, and how do you want it to look? Lay it out, develop a plan, and then take action.

5. Be patient.

One of the most common negative attitudes people harbor is unhappiness with their present circumstances. Be careful not to look so much to the future that you loathe your present. Why be bothered by where you are today if it's part of where you'll be tomorrow?

The mind always searches for what it does not possess. The child who has all the toys wants the one another child has! The young valet dreams about driving the cars of the hotel guests. But those same guests want to make more money this year than last! There is an endless search for attainment. True fulfillment comes by seeing your present through gratitude and hope. Patiently enjoy where you are now, but don't set up camp there. You have to be ready when it's time to move on.

A RESULT OF YOUR ATTITUDE

Psychologist William James said, *"The greatest discovery of my generation is that people can alter their lives by altering their attitudes of mind."* By changing your attitude, you can change anything about yourself that needs to be changed.

During a study of 16,000 executives, particular character traits emerged that defined high achievers (those who generally have a healthy, positive attitude) and low achievers (those who generally have an unhealthy, negative attitude).

- *High achievers cared about people; low achievers were preoccupied with their own security.*
- *High achievers viewed others optimistically; low achievers showed a basic distrust of subordinates and peers.*
- *High achievers sought advice from their subordinates and peers; low achievers did not.*
- *High achievers were listeners; low achievers avoided communication whenever possible.*

If we cut off the negative in life, all that is left is success. Take a close look at your life. *What negative attitudes have you allowed to harbor in your life?* Negative attitudes are like viruses in a computer system. Although they may not effect the computer immediately, in time they will. First, one program crashes. Then another. Then three more. Soon, the whole computer is infected and worthless. All negative attitudes have their sequence of side effects. Stop them now, or they will cripple your life.

> OUR ATTITUDE TOWARD
> LIFE DETERMINES
> LIFE'S ATTITUDE
> TOWARDS US.
> – EARL NIGHTINGALE

Every customer loves an employee who is willing to help. The national chamber of commerce did a study on customer loss and found that sixty-eight percent of customers leave a business because of a bad attitude projected by that business.

If *you* are a businessperson, I want to specifically address you in this chapter. I have some principles to share with you that will help you develop the ethically sound business attitudes you need to launch your business into a new realm of success.

Over the years, I have found that many individuals who are in business should *not* be. They don't know the first thing about how to run a successful business. Every time they step out to try a new venture, they fail; and each time, it not only devastates them financially, but even worse, it destroys their drive.

If *you* are called to be a businessperson, I want to show you how to bring integrity and virtuous conduct into your workplace in such a way that it is both palatable and without compromise. There are things you can do as a businessperson to ensure both continued commerce and a happy work environment. When these principles are practiced, they bring you success in your business and provide a place for you as a leader in your business community. The first principle I want to share with you is very basic: **Servanthood and problem solving produce happy customers.**

> SERVANTHOOD AND
> PROBLEM SOLVING
> PRODUCE
> HAPPY CUSTOMERS.

These two rare qualities not only enrich your personal life, but they also set you apart from the crowd and become your distinction.

The ability to relate with others is an important commodity. Developing your skills in dealing with them must be your primary goal. Your potential for developing leadership skills and a heart for people is much more valuable than the possible amount of money you can make. *It is your service to others that creates the personal wealth you want to obtain.*

Do not rely on negotiating skills and shrewd business strategies to drive your pursuit for success. Instead, allow your *servanthood toward people* to determine your increase. Finances (as long as they are honestly gained) are only an indication of the service and the types of problems you are willing to solve for others.

The lack of servanthood in the business realm is one of the greatest problems we face today. It has its root in *wrong attitudes*.

Every ethical businessperson is required to be a servant; however, in the everyday routine of running a business, too often a person's attitude *does not* reflect a desire to serve others. In fact, he may even act as if people owe *him* something.

You are there to serve people in your industry. It is very difficult for potential clients to reject you when you approach them in humility and

> ATTITUDES IN BUSINESS MUST ALWAYS REFLECT A STRONG DESIRE TO SERVE.

say, "I'm here to serve you and to make life better for you."

Money is the reward for solving problems for your clientele. That means you determine the amount of your income.

DEVELOP A "WIN-WIN" ATTITUDE

You were created and designed for success. **The formula for success always begins with a "win-win" attitude.**

If you are an honorable businessperson, you *and* your clients should always walk away happy, feeling like you both made the greatest deal on the face of the earth.

Many business people have not mastered this "win-win" attitude. They are discouraged by failure, and thus live by excuses, as they wait for a "big breakthrough" to come and change their business for the better in one fell swoop.

"Big breakthroughs" do not happen apart from your participation! Your business "breakthrough" comes as a result of long-term consistency and diligence in applying sound, ethical business principles.

Maxwell Maltz spoke of the fallacy of the "big breakthrough" mentality: *"What is opportunity, and when does it knock? It never knocks. You can wait a*

> CONSISTENCY MAKES YOU SIGNIFICANT AND IS A DETERMINING FACTOR IN A PROSPEROUS FUTURE.

whole lifetime, listening, hoping, and you will hear no knocking. None at all.

You are opportunity, and you must knock on the door leading to your destiny. You prepare yourself to recognize opportunity, to pursue and seize opportunity, as you develop the strength of your personality, and build a self-image with which you are able to live — with your self-respect alive and growing."

KNOW YOUR CLIMATE

Here is what I always say to business people to whom I speak: **Know your business climate, and your new direction will emerge.**

You must understand the financial, consumer, and business climates in which you operate. Let me give you an example. For a number of years, people wrote letters or talked to me about expanding the scope and outreach of this organization to a national level through television and other means. Although I received all this outside counsel, I chose to wait. I understood that the right move at the wrong time is the wrong move. **If you will wait for proper timing, it will transport you to your desired destination.**

> KNOW YOUR BUSINESS CLIMATE, AND YOUR NEW DIRECTION WILL EMERGE.

A lot of business people launch out in such a way that they leave no possibility for retreat in case they encounter the need to back up and make adjustments. They begin their venture without understanding what it will cost to maintain the new level to which they're heading. As a result, they embarrass themselves when they get halfway out and find they can neither go forward nor make the return trip. They cannot finish the work they started because the cost "suddenly" became greater than they anticipated.

That situation may sound all too familiar to you. **Knowing your**

**limitations will keep you from ventur-
ing into the land of business failure.**

You may think, *"If I just go a little bit
further and risk a little bit more, the return
is going to be better."* Not necessarily!
Take your time — don't get in a hurry.
Don't put the proverbial cart in front of
the horse!

> KNOWING
> YOUR LIMITATIONS
> WILL KEEP YOU FROM
> VENTURING INTO
> THE LAND OF
> BUSINESS FAILURE.

Understand the climate in which you live. Understand your own limitations and abilities. Give yourself the chance to master your challenges.
There is nothing wrong with taking a half step at a time. Don't try to hit
a grand slam every time you get up to the plate!

Make sure you have a clear picture of where you are going. I call it
your inner portrait. Never try to out-perform your inner self-portrait —
if you do, you will be frustrated. When you *see* yourself as able to maintain your current level, then it's time to move up. It is also at this point
when *others* (including your authorities) see that you are ready.

This is one principle I understand well. Sometimes I move so slowly
and so circumspectly that many think I'm doing nothing. But, *I never go
backwards.* I never have to retreat, because **I only move forward when I
know I am ready and the timing is right.**

So take your time as you strive to build your business. Slow down.
Don't attempt to enter your future until you use up all of your present. Stop
allowing yourself to get impatient and frustrated. If you get out further
than you can handle, you will not be able to sustain it. If you just continue to *press* (not pry or ramrod) yourself into your future, you will
walk right into it.

Instead of always needing a miracle to bail you out of some miscalcu-
lated situation, take a small step; then put your stake in the ground. Then
take another small step, and put another stake in the ground. It may seem
that this method takes too much time, but I promise you that it is a much

more effective way to successfully reach your goals! Abraham Lincoln affirmed the wisdom of this approach when he said, "*I am a slow walker, but I never walk backwards.*"

I may seem slow, but I always make sure that I have the money to move forward **before** I ever launch out into a new level of growth. For instance, when our corporation decided to expand into television, we had enough cash to pay for the programming a year in advance.

Do not go out further than you can see. Take your time. Then you can *build* your business with success instead of living on the edge. If you must invest everything you have to take the next step, you are in danger. What will you do if you need to step back and adjust your strategy? What will you do when you encounter setbacks?

Now, I realize that many success gurus advocate "going for broke" to gain financial stability. But most people who go for broke do just that — they go broke—permanently!

> DON'T GET IN A HURRY. CAREFULLY CONSIDER THE TIMING FOR EXPANSION AND GROWTH.

So let's review what I've said so far about building your business successfully:

- *Don't get in a hurry. Carefully consider the timing for expansion and growth.*
- *Understand your limitations, but continue to see yourself as a success.*
- *Do not try to go beyond the way you view yourself at any given time.*
- *When you can see yourself successfully maintaining a higher level, move on up to it.*

BECOME THE EXPERT IN YOUR CHOSEN FIELD

What do you really want to achieve in life? Once you discover it, do whatever it takes to excel at it.

Work on becoming the best at what you do. Don't just work with the attitude "Hey, this will make me some money. It's a living." No — go to the top!

Be single-minded in passionate pursuit of excellence in the field of business you have chosen. Remember, "just good enough" never is!

Always combine your excellence with ethics as you pursue success in your field. As you do, you understand the wisest course to take at every turn.

WHAT ABOUT THE PRESENT?

If you are someone who dreams big dreams, realize **success is only a dream to those who talk about it for the future. It is a reality to those who pursue it in the present.**

A lot of people talk about the great things they are going to achieve when they get older, but never really do anything to prepare. Certainly every one of us needs to have a vision to fulfill, a goal to pursue, a dream to achieve. But a dream is worthless if we just talk about it and never do anything.

Henry Miller observed, *"What distinguishes the majority of men from the few is their inability to act according to their beliefs."* As you put your plan into

> SUCCESS IS ONLY A DREAM TO THOSE WHO TALK ABOUT IT FOR THE FUTURE. IT IS A REALITY TO THOSE WHO PURSUE IT IN THE PRESENT.

action *in the present,* you lay the foundation for your dream to be fulfilled in the future.

STAY HONEST WITH YOURSELF

There is no bigger liar than the man who lies to himself. It is common for business people to lie or exaggerate their achievements. Eventually they lie, not only to themselves, but also to others.

Be truthful about your successes and challenges. Truth and honesty, both to yourself and to others, are prerequisites for prosperity and increase in your business, as well as in your personal life. Nathaniel Hawthorne maintained, *"No man, for any considerable period, can wear one face to himself, and another to the multitude, without finally getting bewildered as to which may be true."*

THE POWER OF ASSOCIATION

Take the time to answer the following questions honestly. Find out if you want to be like those with whom you associate closely. If you're not

> FRIENDS
> ARE LIKE BUTTONS ON
> AN ELEVATOR; SOME
> TAKE YOU UP WHILE
> OTHERS TAKE YOU DOWN.

hanging around people you *want to be like,* decide to change your company! You will be glad you did. Remember this proverb, *"He who walks with wise men will be wise, but the companion of fools will be destroyed."*

- *With what kind of people do you associate?*
- *Are they successful in their chosen field?*
- *Are they individuals who strive for excellence?*

This principle highlights the importance of your everyday relationships to determine the outcome of your business and, indeed, your life.

Of course, you should always be kind and helpful with whomever you interact, but don't allow everyone you meet into your personal life. Not every person should hear your secret dreams. Tell your dreams to the wrong people, and you can end up in a lot of trouble! I only share my dreams with those who are closest to me, those friends who can discern what my circumstances might say to me. These are the people who can best encourage me and help me determine the next wise move to fulfill my assignment.

Do you have standards for those you allow access to you? Whether or not you know it, **you suffer both the consequences and the rewards of those who are closest to you.**

> YOU SUFFER BOTH THE CONSEQUENCES AND THE REWARDS OF THOSE WHO ARE CLOSEST TO YOU.

Consider this proverb: *"Faithful are the wounds of a friend, but the kisses of an enemy are deceitful."*

Most people look for others who will accept them in their foolishness. They associate friendship with *comfort*. But friendship and comfort are not the same thing. True friendship is not comfortable. A true friend loves you too much to let you walk in mediocrity. He consistently prods you to *create*, not *coast*. **I would rather have you hate me for telling you the truth than love me for telling you lies!**

True friendship means I trust someone enough to let him pull the splinter out of my eye, without worrying that he will hit me with a two-by-four that's stuck in his own eye! In other words, I know my friend will not point his finger at me in an effort to cover his own shortcomings.

My friend is the kind of person who tolerates nothing but excellence in every area of his life and mine. This is the kind of person I want to try to be like; therefore, this is the kind of friend I allow to walk alongside me through life.

BE WILLING TO DO THE "DIRTY WORK"

As your responsibilities grow, you may become tempted to delegate them. Don't pass off your dirty work to your subordinates. Don't delegate the responsibilities that are rightfully yours to fulfill. **Never ask anyone to perform a task only you can perform.**

One of my staff members recently said to me, "I know you have a lot going on in your responsibilities with this organization. Is there anything I can do to take some of that load off your shoulders?"

"Honestly," I said, "there really isn't anything you can do. Every one of the things I face, I must face alone."

I will not relinquish my responsibilities. They are mine alone. I am not going to push off those responsibilities on someone else so that, just in case the outcome isn't what I expect, I can blame that person instead of myself.

Now, that doesn't mean you're supposed to do everything by yourself. As a businessperson, you need to pass on some tasks to those who faithfully serve you — but not the responsibilities that only you should handle.

NEGATIVE THOUGHTS

Your *thought life* not only affects your business — it affects every area of your life. Do you continually entertain negative thought patterns, playing out scenarios of how things could go *wrong?*

Negative thought patterns *draw* negative situations toward you! If you want to see yourself winning in life and prospering in business, you must replace those negative thoughts by embracing positive thoughts. **The only way to defeat negative thoughts is by focusing on positive ones.**

When you wake up in the morning, expect every aspect of your business to thrive and grow. This creates a posture for success. *Replace* destructive, worrisome thoughts with positive thoughts of winning. *Say* to yourself, *"It doesn't matter how long it takes. It doesn't matter what it looks like on the way. I will stay true to my integrity. I will stay true to my principles. I will stay true to my word. I won't allow any form of compromise to infiltrate my thoughts or my life."*

Do this and see your dreams for success and promotion fulfilled!

CONTROL YOUR EMOTIONS

As important as passion is to success, it is only a tool in your hand, not a compass for your life. You cannot afford to live, walk, and make decisions based upon your emotions. Typically, your mind and emotions run wild when you face difficult challenges in your business. It is detrimental to let your judgment be controlled by the way you feel.

Many times emotions are unstable and quite unpredictable; so those who live by them tend to be the same. Keep your emotions under lock and key as you continue to consistently do the right thing every day. **Learn to live by principle, not emotions!**

Very few people know how to live this way. But those who discipline themselves to think right, to control their emotions and live by ethical principles, move on to success.

Responsibility is personal. You have *a personal responsibility* to grow, to win, and to succeed. No man will do this for you. **Your success is completely dependent upon you.**

COUNT THE COST

To begin any new business venture requires a great deal of sacrifice and personal cost. There is no way around it.

I know many business people whom I consider to be very successful in what they do. I know others who are only moderately successful. Then there are those whom I call "wanna-be's" — those who want to be successful but are not. In fact, the "wanna-be's" talk more about success than do those who are actually very successful!

> THE PRICE OF FUTURE SUCCESS IS THE SACRIFICE OF TODAY'S PLEASURES.

Do you know what usually separates the "wanna-be's" from the authentically successful? It's the four-letter word: *pain.*

The difference between achievers and dreamers is the willingness to sacrifice temporary pleasure and bear pain. It takes pain to succeed, so it's important to ask yourself, *"Am I willing to pay the price?"* Jesus said it well when He asked: *"For which of you, intending to build a tower, does not sit down first and count the cost, whether he has enough to finish it?"*

Count the cost of your business venture — and the cost of it is *pain.* You do not find success by taking the "popularity road" or the road of least resistance. **Success is not your destination if you travel the road of compromise or lower standards.**

> SUCCESS IS A LITTLE MORE THAN THE WILLINGNESS TO BEAR PAIN.

When you determine to succeed, you *will* experience rejection, criticism, scrutiny, and betrayal! You will have people talk about you. Those around you will say you're crazy for thinking the way you do. But if you have an internal mandate and resolve about taking that step, you will endure the rejection and criticism. **Criticism is restricted to the power you give it.**

You may as well accept now that success makes some people critical of you. When you're a failure at what you do, no one is critical of you. In fact, people like you. You're the "good ol' boy who is down on his luck like the rest of us." But as you begin to succeed, you have more critics and fewer pals. Only those who need your services or who understand success seek your company. So just remember — do not allow criticism to have *any* power over you!

> CRITICISM IS RESTRICTED TO THE POWER YOU GIVE IT.

You also must count the cost of financial sacrifice, as you put together the necessary capital to make the business work. This endeavor can be painful along the way to success.

Nevertheless, *don't quit.* Stay *persistent* and *consistent.* Most people who are considered failures did not actually fail; they just quit trying. In the words of Thomas Edison, *"Many of life's failures are people who did not realize how close they were to success when they gave up."*

You are a success, not based on how much money you produce on the outside, but based on the character and fortitude that reside on the inside. Be convinced that you *always* triumph in every situation! Believe you were created for success!

Think of yourself as a gold miner as you press through the pain and the sacrifice of building your business. It may seem like you have to sift through the empty ore forever to hit the vein of gold for which you've been looking. But hold on to your persistent determination not to quit. Just keep sifting until you hit pay dirt!

U.S. President Calvin Coolidge spoke these words concerning persistence: *"Nothing in the world can take the place of persistence. Talent will not; nothing is more common than unsuccessful men with talent. Genius will not; unrewarded genius is almost a proverb. Education will not; the world is full of educated derelicts. Persistence and determination alone are omnipotent."*

> MY TOMORROWS
> ARE ONLY AS BRIGHT
> AS THE PRINCIPLES
> I EMBRACE TODAY.

Success truly is the result of your willingness to bear pain. It is painful to invest all you have into building your business, only to break even or have a very small percentage of profit. But don't fret. Years of prosperity and abundant blessing are coming if you embrace these proven principles. Always keep this in mind: **My tomorrows are only as bright as the principles I embrace today.**

EMPLOYER-EMPLOYEE RELATIONSHIPS

Now I want to address the issue of employer-employee relationships. How you treat your employees is a key to building and maintaining a successful business.

You need to understand that your employees are assigned to help you multiply your business. Because they have such an important role in attaining your business goals, these people are worthy of fair compensation. As an ethical employer, **always pay others what is just and fair in accordance with the problems they solve for you.**

It is always better to overpay your employees than to underpay them. That doesn't mean you should allow the payroll to eat dangerously into your profits. But your employees need to be paid *well* for their work to help you multiply your business.

Speak kindly to them as you give them their instructions. Do not yell or breathe threats if things aren't done the way you like. Every so often, make out two checks for each employee on the regular payday – one for their regular wages and one just to appreciate them. **There is no replacement for kindness and graciousness to others.**

The nature of your relationship with your employees makes or breaks your business in many ways. When your employees are happy, your customers are happy. And when your customers are happy, you are happy, because then your business begins to prosper and expand!

BE ENTHUSIASTIC!

Get excited about the company for which you work! Be excited about your plans, goals, and accomplishments. Your enthusiasm displays your outlook on life.

I have a friend who has a plaque with a motto hanging on the wall behind his desk. It says this: *"Get enthusiastic within ten seconds, or get out of here."* You know,

> ENTHUSIASM IS THE FUEL THAT PROPELS YOU INTO A SUCCESSFUL FUTURE!

that is absolutely true! You should get excited about what you do or get out of it. I'm not talking to you as a person who wants to make a living; I'm talking to you as one who wants to change a generation.

Beyond simply making a buck, your higher aspiration should be to make a mark on your world — to influence this generation. To me, that is the real challenge. But remember, every challenge offers a reward.

There are always spoils to a war. So go out and conquer! Become the best you can be in the business world. Remember these words of Wilfred A. Peterson: *"Success is focusing the full power of all you are in what you have a burning desire to achieve."*

FINAL GUIDELINES

Let's recap the tools we've discussed for building a business that thrives:

- Develop the heart of a servant.
- Count the cost.
- Be careful with whom you associate.
- Become the best at what you do.
- Don't break your word.
- Be true to yourself and truthful to others.
- Stay focused.
- Manage your emotions and thought life.
- Tangibly and generously appreciate your employees.
- Always keep in mind that your *attitude determines your altitude*.

As you follow all these basic guidelines, you will find yourself building toward success, not only in your business, but also in every area of life!

CHAPTER TEN SUMMARY

- Remember, people are your greatest commodity. Developing your skills in dealing with them must be your primary goal. Your potential for developing leadership skills and a heart for people is much more valuable than the possible amount of money you can make.

- Every ethical businessperson is required to be a servant; however, in the everyday routine of running a business, too often a person's attitude does not reflect a desire to serve others.

- Understand the climate in which you live. Understand your own limitations and abilities. Give yourself the chance to master your challenges. There is nothing wrong with taking a half step at a time.

- What do you really want to achieve in life? Once you discover it, do whatever it takes to excel at it. Work on becoming the best at what you do. Don't just work with the attitude "Hey, this will make me some money. It's a living." No — go to the top!

- Henry Miller observed, *"What distinguishes the majority of men from the few is their inability to act according to their beliefs."*

- Consider this proverb: *"Faithful are the wounds of a friend, but the kisses of an enemy are deceitful."*

- Your thought life not only affects your business — it affects every area of your life.

- Responsibility is personal. You have a personal responsibility to grow, to win, and to succeed. No man will do this for you. Your success is completely dependent upon you.

- Do you know what usually separates the "wanna-be's" from the authentically successful? It's the four-letter word: *pain*.

- You are a success, not based on how much money you produce on the outside, but based on the character and fortitude that reside on the inside.

- Get excited about the company for which you work! Be excited about your plans, goals, and accomplishments. Your enthusiasm displays your outlook on life.

- Become the best you can be in the business world. Remember these words of Wilfred A. Peterson: *"Success is focusing the full power of all you are in what you have a burning desire to achieve."*

PRINCIPLES FOR ATTITUDE

* Servanthood And Problem Solving Produce Happy Customers.

* Service To Others Manifests The By-Product Of Personal Wealth.

* Attitudes In Business Must Always Reflect A Strong Desire To Serve.

* The Formula For Success Always Begins With A "Win-Win" Attitude.

* Consistency Makes You Significant And Is A Determining Factor In A Prosperous Future.

* Know Your Business Climate, And Your New Direction Will Emerge.

* Wait For Proper Timing: It Is Transportation To Your Destination.

* Knowing Your Limitations Keeps You From Venturing Into The Land Of Business Failure.

* There Is No Substitute For Becoming The Expert In Your Chosen Field Of Endeavor.

* Excellence Is The Perfume Of A Conscientious Life.

* Success Is Only A Dream To Those Who Talk About It For The Future. It Is A Reality To Those Who Pursue It In The Present.

* There Is No Bigger Liar In Life Than The Man Who Lies To Himself.

* Friends Are Like Buttons On An Elevator; Some Take You Up While Others Take You Down.

* You Suffer Both The Consequences And The Rewards Of Those Who Are The Closest To You.

* I Would Rather Have You Hate Me For Telling You The Truth, Than Love Me For Telling You Lies.

* Never Ask Anyone To Perform A Task That Only You Can Perform.

* The Only Way To Defeat Negative Thoughts Is By Focusing On Positive Ones.

- → Emotions Are Wonderful To Feel With, But Horrible To Live By.

- → The Price Of Future Success Is The Sacrifice Of Today's Pleasures.

- → Success Is Little More Than The Willingness To Bear Pain.

- → Criticism Is Restricted To The Power You Give It.

- → My Tomorrows Are Only As Bright As The Principles I Embrace Today.

- → Always Pay Others What Is Just And Fair, In Accordance With The Problems They Solve For You

- → It Is Difficult To Find A Replacement For Being Kind And Gracious.

Purpose:
Fulfilling Your Destiny
At Work

YOUR PURPOSE IN LIFE
SIGNIFICANTLY DICTATES YOUR
FULFILLMENT IN LIFE.

Many people seek direction for their career, marriage, children, and future. While they scurry around trying to discover their assignments, wisdom quietly tries to tell them, "Just concentrate on fulfilling what's in front of you first, and you'll do just fine!"

So here is the final question we are going to discuss: *What is your assignment in the workplace?* What is your *purpose* to get up and go to work every day?

People have countless reasons for why they pursue a career. They want to go to work so they can:
- Become somebody in life.
- Gain status in the eyes of others.
- Buy a new house, a new car, a new boat, etc.
- Plan an exciting vacation.
- Put their children through private school.

- Enjoy a higher standard of living.
- Boast of their lifetime accomplishments.
- Give their children a better life than they had growing up.

Most employees are more excited about their vacations or time off than about their jobs. With this attitude, it's no wonder some of the most prosperous nations have quickly gone from creditor nations to massively debt-ridden nations.

Many so-called "wealthy" nations and "prosperous" people owe others much more money, proportionately, than their less privileged counterparts. What has caused this downward spiral?

WORK TO GIVE

This is something for which I began searching years ago. I pondered, *Why do I really go to work? Because I enjoy the long hours at my workplace? Because I will be able to buy that extra car? I can only drive so many cars and live in so many houses! So what is this chase all about – why strive to achieve in the workplace at all?*

I found my answer in the writings of the apostle Paul:

> "LET HIM WHO STOLE STEAL NO LONGER, BUT RATHER LET HIM LABOR, WORKING WITH HIS HANDS WHAT IS GOOD, THAT HE MAY HAVE SOMETHING TO GIVE HIM WHO HAS NEED."

First, notice the beginning of this verse, where it says, "*Let him who stole steal no longer....*" How do we steal from our employers?

- **We steal time from our employers when our body is at the office, but our heart is at the lake.**
- **We steal value from our employers when we spend part of our time on the job being idle.**

- *We steal joy from our employers by criticizing them in front of our co-workers.*
- *We steal money from our employers when we "borrow" office supplies and "forget" to return them.*

> GIVE OTHERS MORE THAN THEY REQUIRE, PRESS ON AND GIVE THEM WHAT THEY DESIRE.

This is, in essence, what I learned: *Give others more than they require by giving them what they desire.*

Now look at the rest of what Paul had to say,

"...WORKING WITH HIS HANDS WHAT IS GOOD, THAT HE MAY HAVE SOMETHING TO GIVE HIM WHO HAS NEED."

Go to work every day as though you have something good to give.

The less you go to work, the less you have to give. The more you are motivated by a *bigger purpose* for your work (beyond buying that new boat or new house), the happier you become. You begin to arrive a little earlier and leave a little later. You stop getting involved in all the strife and stress of discontented gossip. In fact, you are happy you can solve problems for your employer and your co-workers. You won't go to your job just to work for yourself anymore. Your motivation changes; you just want to give to others!

You begin to understand that your desire to succeed is fueled by your longing to help *others* succeed. You learn principles of prosperity, not for yourself

> YOU GO TO WORK TO ADD TO OTHERS, NOT TO USE OTHERS.

alone, but to become a template for your children and children's children.

When your purpose for work changes, you begin to draw your affirmation not on the successes or setbacks from your business or workplace, but from your driving desire — to give, to help, to bless others. Then, you don't get so upset when you feel slighted or passed over for a promotion.

When your motivation is to add value, no one can ever take advantage of you. Things that once upset you are not that important anymore. You are free from pettiness, because you learned how to tap into a higher reason for being in the workplace!

UNDERSTANDING AUTHORITY

The first person you should desire to please and *add value* to is your employer. Why is it so difficult for people to focus on pleasing their employers? Because they don't understand the concept of *authority*.

Many individuals do not understand that an authority is approached differently than an acquaintance. Every relationship demands a different posture. **Life contains two orders of people – those whom you are created to please and those whose assignment is to please you.**

It's popular for people to discuss issues with their superiors; "open-door policies" are touted in many businesses these days. However, most employees want to talk about their superior's instructions with one goal in mind — to get their own way.

> LIFE CONTAINS TWO ORDERS OF PEOPLE— THOSE WHOM YOU ARE CREATED TO PLEASE AND THOSE WHOSE ASSIGNMENT IS TO PLEASE YOU.

Yes, dialogue in the workplace is currently very popular. But there is a danger with all this dialogue. The more people talk about an issue, the more confused things seem to get.

You may not agree with your supervisor's decision, but **compliance is honorable, even in the midst of poor decisions.**

If you are going to achieve your goal for promotion, you must point your life in that direction. You will never be promoted at your job if you talk to the other employees about your employer's "bad" decisions.

Get smart about your job. Embrace your employer, not your co-workers. Disgruntled co-workers aren't going to do a thing for you. Here is a good guideline: **Never take an instruction from someone who is unqualified to give you a promotion.**

Will you be criticized when you embrace upward? Yes, most certainly. However, you are only criticized by the people who are not growing. You must *eagerly* pursue pleasing your authorities. A smile should come to their face every time they think of you!

> NEVER TAKE
> AN INSTRUCTION
> FROM ANYONE WHO IS
> UNQUALIFIED TO GIVE
> YOU A PROMOTION.

Go to your supervisor and say, "Sir [or Ma'am], I'm asking you to tell me three things I can do that will please you. How can I do better? What can I do to be more pleasing to you?" Then focus on your performance based on your supervisor's answer.

As I mentioned earlier, promotion comes much more readily when we do more than is expected of us in the workplace. **Promotion is never achieved by only doing what is required, but rather by discovering what is desired of us.**

What you do outside of your job description brings you more than your paycheck can ever give you. A true servant seeks to go beyond the *obligations* of his job description. He finds his deepest fulfillment in *bringing pleasure* to the one he serves; pleasing his

> PROMOTION IS NEVER
> ACHIEVED BY ONLY
> DOING WHAT IS REQUIRED
> OF US, BUT RATHER
> BY DISCOVERING
> WHAT IS DESIRED OF US.

employer actually *energizes him*! He understands that true success lies behind his ability to *please the one who hired him*.

You can see why it takes much more than just desire to go to another level at your job! Go beyond your normal responsibilities and give your employer your loyalty, your faithfulness, and your diligence. No matter what he desires, be willing to do it; then wait for your promotion!

INNER PROSPERITY

Don't let obstacles talk louder than your walk of integrity and persever-ance. No matter what is thrown at you, always endure to the end. Become a person who will not be denied! As you choose the route of excellence, you will be criticized.

"Here comes the 'boss's pet.' He's just 'kissing up' to the boss all the time. I know how to get rid of him — here's what we'll do. We'll all point the finger at him."

Of course, anyone who "kisses up" or seeks to please his authority *will* be the favorite. Do you know any *successful* people in life who sur-round themselves with "Judas" types or betrayers? Of course not!

As you go through the gauntlet of criticism, you may think, *"Maybe I shouldn't be as compliant and pleasing to the boss. Maybe I should be more like my co-workers — resistant and rebellious, challenging his authority when I don't like what he says."*

At this point, you must determine to stick it out. Do what is *difficult but right*, not what is *easy but wrong*. Resolve that you will continue to walk in integrity and follow your internal fortitude. Choose to operate according to these principles: Be willing to do whatever your employer asks of you — do it right, do it fast, and do it with a smile.

Make the decision to be the kind of person to whom Thomas Paine referred when he wrote these words: *"I love the man that can smile in trou-ble, that can gather strength from distress, and grow brave by reflection. 'Tis the business of little minds to shrink; but he whose heart is firm, and whose conscience approves his conduct, will pursue his principles unto death."*

The result of this decision is that you set yourself on a course to success in the midst of amazing odds. Your favor *with those who can promote you* multiplies, and your rewards increase.

As you live by these principles of integrity, you are one step above your colleagues, as you keep moving upward in favor with your authority.

COMPLETION:
YOUR ATTENTION-GETTING ADVANTAGE

Do you know people who start projects but never finish them? That is one of the greatest frustrations any employer experiences — employees who want to be paid a good wage, yet never quite complete the tasks they have been assigned to do.

You must be a finisher. Here is a vital key to victory: **Immediate attention to detail demands the immediate attention of the one you seek to please.**

When you pay attention to the small details, you never fail in the big things in life. Here is an interesting proverb: It is *"...the **little** foxes that spoil the vine."*

Be assured of this: An employee that does not finish his assignments never becomes his employer's "go-to" person.

> IMMEDIATE ATTENTION
> TO DETAIL DEMANDS
> THE IMMEDIATE ATTENTION
> OF THE ONE YOU
> SEEK TO PLEASE.

When an employer is consistently forced to look in other directions for the help he needs, sooner or later he makes one of these three choices:

1) He fires the employee for being a poor worker.

2) He does it himself.

3) He looks elsewhere for the one who will fulfill his vision.

So, the quality that gets your employer's attention is not your friendliness or pleasant mannerisms. The quality that makes you stand out from the rest of your co-workers is finishing. No matter what you are instructed to do, do it well and to completion. **It is foolish to look for another instruction until you have successfully completed your last one.**

> IT IS FOOLISH TO LOOK FOR ANOTHER INSTRUCTION UNTIL YOU HAVE SUCCESSFULLY COMPLETED YOUR LAST ONE.

Many times people want another instruction without finishing the last instruction they were given.

They say, "I just want to know what I can do to get my boss's attention." What was the last thing he told you to do?

"Well, he told me to do this. But I want to hear something else from him."

No, wait a minute. Your employer isn't going say, "Oh, you didn't like my first plan? I'm sorry — here, why don't you try something else?"

No, if he cannot get you to simply do what he has assigned you, he will likely give the next assignment to someone else.

TAKING PERSONAL RESPONSIBILITY

Even when your work ethic and faithful completions bring favor in your direction, it does not mean you immediately will be put in charge. Your supervisor will take some time to observe your performance.

He looks for consistency. "Was this a lucky shot or can this guy do it again?" he asks. "Can he do the menial tasks within the organization, or is he only interested in the spotlight?" You must be found faithful over a little before you are put in charge over much.

It doesn't matter who else is involved in the situation. Take personal responsibility. Do not allow yourself to be affected by what some perceive as unfair treatment.

Do you realize that advancement never happens if you are a bitter person? Prosperity cannot come from a heart that harbors bitterness and offense.

> SOMEONE IS ALWAYS WATCHING YOU WHO CAN RADICALLY AND INSTANTLY CHANGE YOUR FUTURE.

Indeed, it may appear that your employer does not like you, that your fellow co-workers constantly plot against you, and that you have no promise of a future. But hold on. Your promise will come. Eventually, you will *find favor* in your employer's sight. **Someone is always watching you who can radically and instantly change your future.**

GET RID OF ALL RESISTANCE IN YOUR HEART

It's so refreshing and rare to find a softhearted employee. "But my supervisor didn't include me in his planning meetings." That's fine; obviously you didn't need to be involved.

"Do you mean it doesn't bother you when you're not included in important meetings like that?"

No, it doesn't. I'll be involved when my supervisor decides he wants my input. Until that day, I won't be

> NEVER ATTEMPT TO TAKE AUTHORITY OVER SOMETHING FOR WHICH YOU ARE NOT RESPONSIBLE.

involved and I'm happy not to be. **Never atempt to take authority over something for which you are not responsible.**

I will only take responsibility for something when I'm ready and when authority is freely given to me. There are certain things in life for which I will never be responsible. But there are people to whom I'll always be responsible.

A softhearted person — one with no resistance — is a person who can be trusted, because he has no hidden agenda. An employer can be transparent with him because a person like that will not take advantage of his employer. He genuinely cares about matters close to his employer's heart.

That is the reason I can turn to any authority figure in my life and say, "Whatever you want me to do, I'll do it. Whatever you don't want me to have, I won't have it. You just tell me what you want."

You may wonder, "Yes, but what if you really want what your authority doesn't want you to have?"

It doesn't matter. If I'm supposed to have it, I will eventually get it — **but I'll never rebel to get it.** My authority will probably wake up in the middle of the night, knowing he's supposed to give it to me. In the meantime, I just remain focused on my purpose — pleasing him and fulfilling my assignment.

You see, I am willing to go through present pain for future pleasure. I will bow my knee now, because I realize I will receive promotion in the future for my willing obedience. I am softhearted. I have no resistance in my heart.

Being a true servant and problem solver has to do with your heart. You begin to think more about those to whom you've been assigned than you think about yourself. You think about the problems *they* face every day; then you begin to solve those problems one at a time, without ever having to be asked.

STANDING UP TO THE TEST

Here is a workplace truism: *The more you try to fix your problems, the more problems you will discover. But the more you solve the problems of others, the more yours get fixed.*

Every problem solver is tested. Situations always arise to test the purity of your servant's heart. Opportunities arise for you to do the wrong thing. Some of those opportunities are presented to you as *shortcuts to your goals.*

It is at this point that you must not only be a *problem solver,* but also *a person of principle.* Choose to stand in your integrity, in spite of great pressure to compromise.

> THE MORE YOU TRY
> TO FIX YOUR PROBLEMS,
> THE MORE PROBLEMS
> YOU WILL DISCOVER.
> BUT THE MORE
> YOU SOLVE THE PROBLEMS
> OF OTHERS, THE MORE
> YOURS GET FIXED.

In order to see favor and promotion flow into your life, demonstrate a keen ability and willingness to overcome and conquer what most men never conquer — your self-will. Say "No!" to compromise, bitterness, strife, anger, and rejection. Determine never to say a word to promote yourself, because a principled problem solver never becomes opportunistic. *And learn how to wait for the day of your promotion.*

CHAPTER ELEVEN SUMMARY

- What is your assignment in the workplace? What is your purpose to get up and go to work every day?

- You begin to understand that your desire to succeed is fueled by your longing to help others succeed. You learn principles of prosperity, not for yourself alone, but to become a template for your children and children's children.

- If you are going to achieve your goal for promotion in the workplace, you must point your life in that direction. You will never be promoted at your job if you talk to the other employees about your employer's "bad" decisions.

- Don't let obstacles talk louder than your walk of integrity and perseverance. No matter what is thrown at you, always endure to the end. Become a person who will not be denied!

- Do you know people who start projects but never finish them? That is one of the greatest frustrations any employer endures — employees who want to be paid a good wage, yet never quite complete the tasks they have been assigned to do.

- So, the quality that gets your employer's attention is not your friendliness or pleasant mannerisms. The quality that makes you stand out from the rest of your co-workers is finishing.

- In order to see favor and promotion flow into your life, you need to demonstrate a keen ability and willingness to overcome and conquer what most men never conquer — your self-will.

- Imagine what would happen in your life if you made the decision to overcome every obstacle and stay faithful until the end. It's completely up to you.

PRINCIPLES FOR PURPOSE

- Give Others More Than They Require, Press On And Give Them What They Desire.

- Work Every Day As Though You Have Something Good To Give.

- You Go To Work To Add To Others, Not To Use Others.

- Understand The Unspoken Chain Of Command, And You Will Discover The Master Rule Of The Universe.

- Life Contains Two Orders Of People — Those Whom You Are Created To Please And Those Whose Assignment Is To Please You.

- Compliance Is Honorable, Even In The Midst Of Poor Decisions.

- Never Take An Instruction From Anyone Who Is Unqualified To Give You A Promotion.

- Promotion Is Never Achieved By Only Doing What Is Required Of Us, But Rather By Discovering What Is Desired Of Us.

- Prosperity Is Never Defined By What A Man Has But By Who A Man Is.

- Immediate Attention To Detail Demands The Immediate Attention Of The One Whom You Seek To Please.

- It Is Foolish To Look For Another Instruction Until You Have Successfully Completed Your Last One.

- In Life You Will Discover That Every Problem Is Personal And Internal.

- Someone Is Always Watching You Who Can Radically And Instantly Change Your Future.

- Never Attempt To Take Authority Over Something You Are Not Responsible For.

- The More You Try To Fix Your Problems, The More Problems You Will Discover. But The More You Solve The Problems Of Others, The More Yours Get Fixed.

Promotion
Is Rightfully Yours

Imagine what your life could become if you live by the principles in this book. Imagine what can happen in *your* life if you make the decision to overcome every obstacle and stay faithful until the end. It's completely up to you.

You can enter your highest poten-tial in your career, business, or place of employment. You just have to deter-mine to pursue excellence and develop

> **ENJOY THE FRUIT OF YOUR LABOR WHERE YOU ARE IN LIFE RIGHT NOW!**

a true servant's heart. Make the decision to become an eager, willing problem solver for those to whom you are assigned. As you journey, make sure to **enjoy the fruit of your labor where you are in life right now!**

Relish every moment of every day, no matter what season of life you are in. If an individual is not grateful, he is not successful, no matter how much money he has! If all you can afford is hamburgers, then buy yourself the best-looking hamburger you can find. Then sit down to eat with the nicest people you can find, and enjoy that hamburger, thankful all the while!

> REAL SUCCESS
> IS THE PRODUCT OF
> A GRATEFUL HEART.

Then, as you move up to steak, and on to filet mignon, keep *savoring* every second of your life. Enjoy the labor of your hands. Don't live in such constant anticipation of your future that you view your present with disdain.

Enjoy where you are at the present moment — but make sure you don't set up camp there! Once again, excellence is not a destination, it's a journey.

QUANTIFIABLE CONTRIBUTION

Ethics, character, respect, personal productivity, and a strong work ethic — these are just some of the tools I've shared with you in this book. **Live by them and your value immediately becomes apparent and measurable. Your distinction and favor in the workplace soar, as do your rewards.**

These principles help you pursue an uncompromising standard of excellence in the workplace. Use these tools to build into your life a solid platform of impeccable character and good work habits. Then, launch off that platform and rise to the next level, winning at work and in every arena of your life!

What Author And Speaker
Dr. Mike Murdock Has To Say

When Robb Thompson speaks, leaders listen.

Recently, I sat at a table surrounded by a select group of leaders well known for their integrity, excellence, influence, and unparalleled productivity. One by one, each leader shared his encounters and experiences with Dr. Robb Thompson. The conclusion was always the same. No one could recall meeting any human with a higher standard of excellence. I understood their profound respect. Robb is the most consistent, giving, and trustworthy friend a person could ever have.

His integrity is impeccable.

His standard of excellence has yet to be surpassed by anyone I have known in my thirty-six years of world travel.

His generosity is legendary...as yet unequaled by any other known leader.

He is the greatest giver I have ever known. He is one of the very few who has mastered both the Law of the Seed and the Law of Excellence, the two greatest laws on earth.

He is the most qualified leader I know to mentor us on the Law of Excellence and Promotion.

He has forever changed my life.

Now…this unforgettable book will forever change your life.

Dr. Mike Murdock

Footnotes

1. Dawson, Roger. *Weekend Millionaire Mindset*. (Magraw-Hill companies, 2005)
2. Josephson, Michael S. Hanson, Wes. *The Power of Character*. (Unlimited Pub. 2004)
3. Proverbs 13:4
4. Proverbs 13:4
5. Proverbs 22:11
6. Proverbs 22:29
7. Proverbs 15:1
8. Proverbs 13:20
9. Proverbs 20:6
10. Mike Murdock, *The Assignment: The Dream & the Destiny, Volume 1* (Denton, TX: The Wisdom Center, 1996), p. 7-10.
11. Mike Murdock, *Seeds of Wisdom on Your Assignment* (Denton, TX: The Wisdom Center, 2001), p. 2.
12. Luke 6:31
13. Proverbs 10:4
14. Proverbs 18:9 (KJV)
15. Luke 16:10 (NIV)

16. Proverbs 13:20
17. Proverbs 27:6
18. Luke 14:28
19. Ephesians 4:28
20. Song of Solomon 2:15

*All unreferenced quotes were taken from Cyber Quotation Database. www.cybernation.org

About Robb Thompson International

Robb Thompson International (RTI) is an organization dedicated to helping people excel in life and maximize their God-given potential. Dedicated to training:

- Corporate Leaders
- Governmental Entities
- Future Leaders
- Individuals

RTI desires to see leaders on a global scale embrace, execute, and operate under three core values: Integrity, Excellence, and Loyalty. RTI seeks to make a positive impact by influencing the highest levels of world leadership including: Presidents, Royalty, Corporate Executives, and Religious Leaders, both nationally and internationally.

Robb Thompson Live!

Dr. Robb Thompson has been called "Today's most compelling and pragmatic speaker." He captivates audiences around the world with principles that are simple, yet profound. Dr. Thompson leaves you with the knowledge and motivation to transform your life and career.

Available for:
- Conferences
- Seminars
- Workshops

To have Dr. Robb Thompson or one of his associates at your next event, call our offices at 708.614.9896 or email justin@robbthompson.com.

Library of Topics:

Your Passport To Promotion

The Unparalleled Power of Problem Solving

Achieving Personal Excellence

Pillars of Leadership

Maximize Your Relationships

And more...

Resources:

Start pressing towards excellence and a higher quality of life! Using the integrated tools and resources developed by Dr. Robb Thompson, you can take control of every facet of your life – achieve optimum financial status, live every day with passion, and master essential life principles. Make a commitment today to hold yourself accountable for your personal growth.

Please visit our website at **www.robbthompson.com.**

ARE YOU READY TO INSPIRE EXCELLENCE IN YOUR LIFE?

"SUCCESS AND FAILURE ARE DESTINED TO NO ONE; THEY ARE **DESTINATIONS** OF A CHOSEN PATH"

DR. ROBB THOMPSON

Now is your opportunity to receive Robb Thompson's Weekly Inspiring Personal Excellence Newsletter.

Robb Thompson, America's leading expert on Personal Excellence, teaches you many subjects such as...

- Excellence: What it is and how you can apply it to your life
- Relationships: The rules and laws that govern all healthy relationships
- Character: The foundation upon which your life stands
- Focus: Learn how to focus on where you are going rather than what you are going through
- The Mind: Learn the latest about how to overcome negative thoughts
- Personal Achievement: How to set goals and establish a personal growth plan
- Respect: Attract everything good to come to your life
- And much, much more sent straight to your inbox...

To receive your free weekly e-newsletter visit our website at **www.robbthompson.com** and click on the link *Inspiring Excellence Newsletter.*

LEADERS UNITED

EXCELLENCE IN BUSINESS INTERNATIONAL is a new, exciting, and unique business association created with you in mind! This association was formed to unite business leaders, including entrepreneurs and corporate executives, in a dynamic network providing information, education, and support. Our desire is for you to experience success, not just in business, but in every area of your life! We are committed to assist you in succeeding financially, relationally, in your community, and in your home.

FULFILLING THE PURPOSE FOR YOUR LIFE becomes possible only when you embrace the right relationships. More than any other ingredient, your relationships determine the outcome of your life. With the right people in your life, there is NO LIMIT to what you are able to accomplish, both personally and professionally.

Because we understand how important networks are to you, we invite you to join Excellence in Business International. Through EBI, you will establish networks with people who are PASSIONATE ABOUT SUCCESS and dedicated to excellence.

In addition to connecting you with like-minded businessmen and businesswomen, joining EBI also makes available to you these benefits:

- Networking opportunities, locally and globally
- Inspirational and informative monthly gatherings
- Business and leadership conferences featuring renowned speakers
- Personal Executive Coaching
- Business Consulting Services
- Management and Employee Training
- Corporate Chaplaincy Services
- Extensive Business and Leadership Resource Library

EXCELLENCE IN BUSINESS INTERNATIONAL

DISCOVER
YOUR TRUE POTENTIAL

Everyone needs a coach in life—someone to encourage you, hold you accountable, challenge you, and **thrust you beyond your potential curve!** Unlike counseling, coaching unlocks your true potential. Personalized coaching has been proven to be the most effective way to cultivate personal and professional skills.

Dr. Robb Thompson is serious about results. After nearly 30 years of learning, mentoring, and teaching simple but life change principles, Dr. Thompson has developed a system of personal transformation that will work for anyone who desires to change.

FOR MORE INFORMATION, CALL OR EMAIL!

708.614.9896
coach@robbthompson.com

ROBB THOMPSON
COACHING